war dogs

Dogs join the military at Front Royal, Virginia, in August 1942. World War II was the first war in which the United States officially brought dogs into the military. Over 10,000 US dogs served during World War II and most were donated to the cause by patriotic civilians who offered their pets for service.

Credit: Courtesy of the US National Archives and Records Administration

war
dogs

TALES OF CANINE HEROISM,
HISTORY, AND LOVE

REBECCA FRANKEL

St. Martin's Press
New York

www.stmartins.com

Design by Letra Libre, Inc.

Library of Congress Cataloging-in-Publication Data

Names: Frankel, Rebecca, author.

Title: War dogs : tales of canine heroism, history, and love / Rebecca Frankel.

Description: New York : St. Martin's Griffin, [2016] | Includes bibliographical references and index.

Identifiers: LCCN 2016016826| ISBN 9781250112286 (trade pbk.) | ISBN 9781250112293 (e-book)

Subjects: LCSH: Dogs—War use—United States. | Dogs—Training. | Iraq War, 2003–2011. | Afghan War, 2001–

Classification: LCC UH100 .F83 2016 | DDC 956.7044/342—dc23

LC record available at https://lccn.loc.gov/2016016826

Our books may be purchased in bulk for promotional, educational, or business use. Please contact your local bookseller or the Macmillan Corporate and Premium Sales Department at 1-800-221-7945, extension 5442, or by e-mail at MacmillanSpecialMarkets@macmillan.com.

First Edition: September 2016

10   9   8   7   6   5   4   3   2   1

contents

Author's Note   vii
The United States at War   xi
Map   xii

Introduction   1

Part One   In the Line of Fire   5

Part Two   Training for War   35

Part Three   What's Love Got to Do with It?   101

Part Four   The Fallen   137

Part Five   More Dogs on Duty   157

Part Six   What Happens When Wars End   191

Part Seven   Home Again, Home Again   199

Acknowledgments   217
Glossary   221
Notes   225
Index   237

People have been trying to understand dogs ever since the beginning of time. One never knows what they'll do. You can read every day where a dog saved the life of a drowning child, or lay down his life for his master. Some people call this loyalty. I don't. I may be wrong, but I call it love—the deepest kind of love. . . .

It's a shame that people all over the world can't have that kind of love in their hearts. . . . There would be no wars, slaughter, or murder; no greed or selfishness. It would be the kind of world that God wants us to have—a wonderful world.

—Wilson Rawls, *Where the Red Fern Grows*

author's note

When I was a kid, I had a habit of "rescuing" animals—though some might have called it kidnapping. There were the neighborhood dogs who for some reason or another were not well looked after and so I would bring them home where I could take care of them. There was the big orange chow who was left in a hot sunny backyard across the street without cold water to drink. There was the beagle from down the block who used to follow me to the bus stop and who would still be there after school to eventually follow me home. Then there was the litter of kittens I found living in the woods at my summer camp who had no one to look after them.

My mother endured whatever strange dog or wounded bird I brought into the yard with good-tempered exasperation while my sister, in a show of sibling solidarity, championed my efforts. But if my affinity for animals comes from anywhere, it is from my father, a Connecticut farm boy who taught me how to befriend a dog, hold a cat, and love all animals and to treat them with dignity and respect.

So in many ways, it's very fitting that so many years after my days of bringing home stray dogs and cats, the first book I would write would be a book about animals. As an editor of *Foreign Policy* magazine, much of my job was spent either writing about world events or working with other journalists on their reported stories from around the world. But part of the work I did involved finding photographs for those stories and so I spent hours going over large collections of images, which included graphic scenes from the wars happening in Afghanistan and Iraq. I'd grown more or less accustomed to seeing the searing reds and whites of rocket-propelled grenade blasts; sand clouds kicked up by Chinook helicopters; the bloodied limbs of soldiers and civilians—all the frozen-by-the-camera moments of anguish and death. Then I found an image of a Marine battalion kicking back at Camp Huskers, located along the outskirts of Marjah, Afghanistan. In the photo, the sunlight slanted warmly over the Marines and the battalion's bomb-sniffing dogs. The dogs were sprawled across the men's laps or curled close against their sides.

This photo surprised me. I was struck by the sense of contentment radiating from these Marines and their dogs. There were no furrowed brows, no Kevlar vests or helmets, no Ray-Ban sunglasses obscuring their eyes. These young men looked tranquil, happy even. The dogs were all but grinning. It evoked a sweet pang of home.

I shared the image with Tom Ricks (a longtime journalist who reported on the Iraq and Afghanistan wars and a great lover of dogs), thinking he might like to post the photograph on *The Best Defense*, his *Foreign Policy* blog. On his suggestion, we began to partner in a new Friday feature we called "Rebecca's War Dog of the Week." He appointed me Chief Canine Correspondent. And so my eyes were opened to the wide world of war dogs.

My biggest fear in stepping into this world was that I felt I had no business in it. I have never held rank in the military. Even as a journalist writing about the policies and events surrounding these wars, or as an editor working with reporters and photo-journalists assigned to cover these regions, I was at best a distant observer. Perhaps I was well informed and well intentioned, but I was still an outsider.

Yet, every time I talked with someone in the Military Working Dog (MWD) community, whether it was a handler on deployment in Iraq, a veterinary technician stationed in Afghanistan, a veteran scout-dog handler from the Vietnam War, or a volunteer for a therapy-dog nonprofit, the barriers I feared might separate us melted away. You don't have to walk a mile down a bomb-laden road in Kandahar, Afghanistan, to know a dog's pull of devotion or the sadness you feel when it becomes clear that the four-legged member of your family is fading and it is time to say good-bye. It's a feeling that goes beyond the individualized experiences that might otherwise put us on distant life paths. To have loved an animal is to share a kinship with others who have loved one too.

I spent three years exploring the world of war dogs for this book. It extends further and wider than I could have imagined, containing communities within communities. It is a place filled with tremendous spirit and solidarity. I thought I would be writing a book about dogs who live their lives in the service of the military. But as much as it is about dogs, this is a book about the mark they leave on their handlers, on their community inside the military, and on all of us who depend on their bravery.

In some ways, I was surprised when I realized I was actually writing a book about people, the people who bear this mark the most deeply. And in the end, that included me as well.

When we cannot make that human connection over war, when we cannot empathize or imagine the far-off world of a combat zone, we can still understand what it means to love a dog. These MWDs are a bridge over the divide that separates military from civilians, participants from onlookers. The stories of military dogs' heroism and sacrifice connect those of us who have no other tie to the battlefields where our servicemen and women are fighting. There is something less complicated (and, ironically, more human) about relating to war through the story of a dog. And, for as long as we have a military made of men and women, we should have military dogs.

A FEW WORDS ABOUT WORDS

As you read this book, you'll notice that some of the military dogs' names begin with two of the same letter. Those are not spelling errors. The US MWD program breeds dogs, and the resulting puppies are identified by names that begin with the same double letter. For example, in June 2010, a litter of Belgian Malinois puppies were born into the "R" litter and were given names that included Rrespect, Rromano, Rruck, and Rrisky.

You'll notice too that when I write of "the handler" or "the working dog" in a general way, I use "he" or "his." I did this just for consistency's sake.

I also made a conscious decision at the beginning of writing this book not to use the pronoun "it" when talking about these dogs. Therefore, they are always "he" or "she." In my mind, "it" refers to a thing, and dogs are not things. They are our feeling and emotionally engaged companions. And, especially as this book shows, they are oftentimes more than that, certainly nothing less.

the United States at war

The following is a list of major conflicts in which the United States has participated:

American Revolutionary War: 1775–1783
War of 1812: 1812–1815
American Civil War: 1861–1865
World War I: 1914–1918*
World War II: 1939–1945†
Korean War: 1950–1953
Vietnam War: 1955–1975‡
Gulf War: 1990–1991
Operation Enduring Freedom, Afghanistan: 2001–2014
War in Iraq (Operation Iraqi Freedom): 2003–2011

---

* Dates of US involvement: 1917–1918
† Dates of US involvement: 1941–1945
‡ Dates of US involvement: 1965–1973

COLORADO
SPRINGS,
COLORADO
Fort Carson
United States
Air Force Kennels

YUMA, ARIZONA
Yuma Proving Ground
The Inter-Service
Advanced Skills K-9 Course

NORTH
AMERICA

SAN ANTONIO, TEXAS
Lackland Air Force Base
Military Working Dog Training School

ATLANTIC
OCEAN

PACIFIC
OCEAN

SOUTH
AMERICA

EUROPE

ASIA

PACIFIC
OCEAN

AFGHANISTAN

IRAQ

FRICA

VIETNAM

INDIAN
OCEAN

AUSTRALIA

Map by Christian Paniagua

introduction

Despite the many distant stars there was no moon, and the night sky was all the blacker for it. The desert air had chilled. You could also feel tensions rising in the village as rapid, loud gunfire crackled down the market lane. A high-pitched hiss sizzled in the distance, followed by the deep shudder of an explosion. *Boom!* Then came another, and another.

Shouts chorused through the cramped alleyway. Someone in the unit had been hit. There was the scuffle of boots, the cries for "Medic!" and the sound of gravel scratching across the ground as soldiers rushed to get to the wounded.

Inside a hut, a group of men huddled around the injured party while the damage was assessed. It was a broken leg, and a bad one at that.

The casualty, though, wasn't one of the people kneeling. It was the dog lying next to them.

Staff Sergeant Fred Roberts, the dog's handler, went to treat his partner's wounds. Turbo, the panicked dog, resisted. He thrashed and twisted. He kicked his hind legs. It took two able-bodied men to hold him down. Roberts was rattled. His hands fumbled over the gauze as he struggled to set the bone and wrap the bandage. Finally, after what felt like many breath-held minutes, the dressing was secure.

Roberts leaned back, sweat slick across his brow. Turbo lay panting, the fight in him subsiding as if he knew the worst was over. And it was, for that night.

What had just taken place had not happened in the throes of a war zone. Instead, it was all part of a carefully staged, pre-deployment training session at the Yuma Proving Ground (YPG), a remote military base in the desert of Yuma, Arizona. There had been no real bullets or explosions. Turbo's injuries and treatment were all pretend, for practice.

I had watched it all, from just a few steps away, with my heart pounding inside my chest. Though it had been just a training exercise, the anxiety and the adrenaline rush of the participants had been real. It was March 2012, and I was observing 17 handler-dog teams take the Inter-Service Advanced Skills K-9 (ISAK) course hosted at YPG. The course was designed to prepare handlers and their dogs from all branches of the military—Marine Corps, Air Force, Army, and Navy—for what awaited them in a combat zone.

YPG, near the California border, stretches 1,300 square miles. Each year, this immense area, which is larger than the entire state of Rhode Island, tests over 10,000 artillery, mortar, and missile rounds. The only other place in the world where you can get such a concentrated amount of explosive material together in one place is a combat zone.

Perhaps Roberts slept better that night, knowing that if his dog was ever hit for real, now he and Turbo would be better prepared to face it.

Roberts and Turbo, and most of the handlers and their dogs attending this particular course, deployed. Many of them went to combat zones. Not all of them returned.

It's not known when the first dog entered the battlefield to wage war alongside his human companions. Historians believe that thousands of years ago the ancient Egyptians used canines to carry messages. The Corinthians surrounded their seashore citadel with guard dogs in 400 BC, and the ancient Romans employed them to raise alarms for their garrisons. The army of Attila the Hun (AD 406–453) brought ferocious hounds with them to protect their camps during battle.

The United States, historically, has been woefully slow to adopt dogs into its military ranks. It did not do so officially until 1942, when the Army's Dogs for Defense program began. So crucial were these animals during World War II that the US canine ranks swelled to over 10,000 dogs strong. During the Vietnam War, US scout dogs thwarted the ambush tactics of the Vietcong so successfully that the Vietcong placed bounties exceeding $20,000 on their heads, twice the amount offered for their human handlers.

In recent years, working outside the wire in Iraq and Afghanistan, military dogs became the single greatest advantage allied forces had against the signature weapon of the post-9/11 era—the improvised explosive device (IED). Although the military has to develop bomb-sniffing technology and electronic machinery, nothing has been more effective at uncovering these lethal roadside bombs than a handler and his detection dog.

Military Working Dogs (MWDs) came most strongly into the public spotlight in May 2011, when Cairo, a dog reportedly attached to a Navy SEAL team, helped take down Osama bin Laden. Bin Laden was the founder of the militant Islamic extremist organization al Qaeda and the mastermind behind the 9/11 attacks. Many of us were exhilarated by the idea that a dog was part of this historic event. When it came time to pull together the world's most capable and specialized military team to hunt down and take out the world's most wanted man, the SEALs made sure an MWD was part of the team.

But what is a war dog exactly? A furry but devoted weapon? A faithful fighter? A fierce soldier? A guardian who keeps watch in the night? A war dog is at once all of these things and still somehow more than the mere sum of those collected roles and qualities. Nothing is as critical or profound as the interdependence and trust between a man and his dog on the battlefield. In combat, where lives are at stake, the capacity for the bond between handler and dog to expand and deepen in intensity and feeling becomes exceptionally great.

The handler and dog relationship is built on a mutual trust that can flourish into something more intimate. It is trust with a great sense of loyalty, and even love. It's this bond that, in a combat zone, encourages a dog's desire to work his keen senses to the advantage of his human companions and inspires heroic feats of bravery when the instinct to flee or the sense of fear might dictate otherwise.

A handler-dog team experiences everything together, including trauma and injuries. But, if it all seems too unendurable, the handler and dog who suffer the same afflictions can even heal together. It is a relationship that challenges and changes the way a person experiences war.

To know war dogs is not to know war, but the dogs can help us understand it better. By recognizing the bond between a handler and his dog, we can see the people at the other end of the leash more clearly. And to know a handler and his dog's lot in war helps us to better understand our military and our country's lot in war. And, just as war dogs save lives, they also enrich them.

part one

in the line of fire

I actually got jealous when I saw some of the soldiers over there with dogs deeply attached to them. It was the nearest thing to civilization in this weird foreign life of ours.

—Ernie Pyle, *Brave Men*

1

As the plane descended, it almost felt like it was falling, but the turns were tight, controlled. The C-17 twisted down, down, down without slowing. The 12 dogs in their crates felt the strange sensation. A few cowered in their kennels, legs splayed, eyes darting and nervous. Some of their handlers gripped their seats. Others closed their eyes, no doubt fighting nausea. The corkscrew landing pattern was a combat zone necessity. So was the short approach to the flight line. The plane, which had left San Diego, California, 20 hours earlier, landed on the Iraq airstrip. It came down so hard and so fast that, as it met the ground, the g-force slapped against the bodies of everyone inside.

When the men stepped off the plane and into the Iraq air, there was nothing but darkness. There was no way to tell where they were. The three Special Forces (SF) guys who had also been on the flight had already melted away into the night.

It was March 2004. Only a couple of days before, Staff Sergeant Sean Lulofs and 11 other Air Force handlers had been at Camp Pendleton in California filling out the necessary paperwork at the Marine Corps base before they could begin their deployment. A lieutenant colonel gave them their first briefing for their mission, Operation Phantom Fury. She did not mince words. "The Marine Corps," she told them, "anticipates that at least two to three of you will be killed in action."

The handlers and their dogs would embed deep within the Marines' infantry units, and it was crucial that the men understood the risks. It would be so dangerous, in fact, that an objective assessment of the mission conducted by the Marine Corps concluded that this group of handlers was expected to come back at a loss.

From the time he was five years old, Lulofs knew he wanted to become a dog handler. His mother had taken him to a police demonstration where they watched an officer place a bag of cocaine in a woman's purse. Then a dog was brought in. Within minutes, the dog found the cocaine. Lulofs knew he'd discovered his life's work.

Staff Sergeant Lulofs had been given less than eight hours' notice that he and his dog Aaslan would be deploying to Iraq. Truth be told, it was the last place in the world he wanted to be. The news of four American contractors who'd been killed there earlier that month had dominated the headlines. The images of a mob pulling charred corpses through the streets then dangling them from a bridge over the Euphrates River were fresh in Lulofs's mind. From the outside, the Iraqis appeared to be full of rage, and they were directing it at Americans.

Now Lulofs and the other handlers stood on the tarmac, in the dark, with no idea where they were. There was a mandatory military blackout, so they couldn't use lights. They hadn't packed night vision goggles (NVGs), because they hadn't known they were going to need them. Lulofs wondered what else they might need that they didn't have. After a few minutes, the men began to load their weapons. Then they heard a deep voice from nearby ask, "Are you the Air Force guys?"

Lulofs felt a twinge of relief. He knew this voice. It was Gunnery Sergeant William Kartune, a rugged, no-nonsense Marine in charge of all the dog teams in Iraq, from Baghdad to Al Anbar. He had come to collect the handlers.

2

After that night, the handlers were split into smaller groups. Lulofs was paired with Joshua Farnsworth, a staff sergeant who seemed to have a big chip on his shoulder. Together they took their dogs to Camp Baharia, located just two miles southeast of the city of Fallujah. Fallujah had become the epicenter of violence. Nobody wanted Fallujah.

The base was so close to the city that Lulofs could see cars on Fallujah's main highway. Before it became Camp Baharia in 2003, the area had been a Ba'ath Party retreat known as Dreamland. Palm trees had surrounded a man-made lake, where the sons of Iraqi dictator Saddam Hussein had watched boats race back and forth across the water.

In the last few months, the area had been torn up by fighting. Many of the buildings had been gutted, including the handlers' living quarters. The glass in the windows had been blown out. Lulofs and another handler found plywood and sandbags and rebuilt walls where needed. They even managed to construct a couple of bunk beds. It was palatial compared to the floor of a Humvee, where some of the other handlers were sleeping.

The first morning, Lulofs woke early, just as the sun was rising. He took Aaslan outside and unclipped his leash to give him free range of the dirt and rock that made up the bank of the lake. Lulofs smiled as he watched the dog sniff around. Aaslan, a trim Belgian Malinois with shadowy dark coloring around his narrow face, had a civil temperament. He never growled at people, never barked at other dogs, and would bite only when asked to, only when he knew it was okay. He was a tough dog, and during bite-work training, Aaslan had hit decoys hard. He once even broke his own legs during a drill. That kind of fight was in his blood. His mother, Boyca, had been legendary for her hardiness. During one training session, she had pounced with such force on a human decoy that even though the man had been wearing a fully padded bite suit, she'd cracked three of his ribs.

Lulofs watched Aaslan skirt the bank, looking for the right spot to do his business. No sooner had Aaslan raised his

US Air Force Staff Sergeant Sean Lulofs on patrol with MWD Aaslan in Iraq in 2004.

Credit: Courtesy of Sean Lulofs

leg when Lulofs saw the dog wrinkle his nose and cock his head to the side. Aaslan paused, leg in the air, and stopped urinating midstream. Lulofs's blood went cold. Aaslan was "on bomb." *But how could that be possible?* Lulofs wondered. They were *inside* the base.

As Lulofs watched, Aaslan began to search, nose to the ground, twisting and sniffing. Lulofs told himself the dog had to be picking up on some kind of residual odor, something left over from unexploded ordnance. He stared in disbelief as Aaslan nuzzled around a coffee can and planted his hindquarters on the ground. "That's not good," Lulofs said to himself. He called Aaslan back to him and away from whatever was in that coffee can.

The Explosive Ordnance Disposal (EOD) team came to investigate. The can looked like a harmless piece of trash. But it was filled with rocks, disarranged wires, and rocket propellant. According to the EOD guys, it had gotten waterlogged after sitting idle for a long time. This made it even more volatile.

The night before, while Lulofs and Farnsworth were making introductions with the Marines on base, they'd hung out in this yard by the water, talking, smoking, shooting the breeze. One of the Marines had a fishing rod, and the guys were casting it out onto the bank to see if they could hook up stray bits of garbage. The thing was, they'd been messing around with this very same coffee can. Lulofs had even taken a picture of one Marine holding it up, a lit cigarette dangling from his lip. They'd had no idea they had been playing with an IED.

The next day, the base was hit with roughly 18 rounds of indirect fire. Lulofs and Aaslan had been in Iraq a grand total of two days, and they were already in the thick of the war, as close to it as they could possibly be.

3

Just 12 months earlier, bombs had rained down on Baghdad. In March 2003, President George W. Bush had stood before the nation and announced that, on his order, coalition forces were going into Iraq to disarm Saddam Hussein and save the world from grave danger. "Our nation enters this conflict reluctantly—yet, our purpose is sure," President Bush informed the world. "The people of the United States and our friends and allies will not live at the mercy of an outlaw regime that threatens the peace with weapons of mass murder. We will meet that threat now, with our Army, Air Force, Navy, Coast Guard and Marines, so that we do not have to meet it later with armies of fire fighters and police and doctors on the streets of our cities."

By late 2003, insurgents' use of IEDs to inflict terror had increased tremendously. Forty to 60 percent of all attacks started with an IED. And these were attacks to which US and coalition forces were extremely vulnerable. How to deal with the IED problem quickly became a top priority. A number of solutions were investigated, and different ideas were teased out and tested. In early 2004, General James Mattis issued an order down the chain of command inside the Marine Corps to investigate whether dogs might be brought in to help with the growing threat.

Was it possible for dogs to become a permanent part of a Marine battalion? Could dogs be attached to a unit? Could they be paired easily with infantrymen? The idea evolved and morphed and eventually the task, and its funding, came under the jurisdiction of the Marine Corps MWD program. The Marine Corps determined that roughly 30 dogs and handlers were needed. They combed their own units, as well as other branches of the military, for the best dog teams available.

It would be almost a full year after the 2003 invasion before the Marines sent dogs to Iraq. Then they deployed six dog teams from their own service along with others from the Air Force. These were the first dog teams flown into a combat area since the Vietnam War. No US dogs had been used in a war as an on-the-ground force in over three decades.

In fact, these dogs and their handlers were law enforcement teams. They had been trained for patrol work. They knew how to search cars, detain suspects, and find drugs and maybe bomb materials. They had not been trained for war. And they were categorically unprepared for what awaited them in Iraq.

They hadn't been trained to conduct roadway searches or to hunt for IEDs. The dogs hadn't been conditioned to search for buried explosives for the simple reason that this specific hazard did not exist stateside, nor had it been a factor in prior conflicts. The first dog handlers in Iraq were basically starting from scratch. They had to make it up as they went along.

4

When Marine handler Corporal Mark Vierig arrived in Iraq in 2004 with his dog, Duc, he knew next to nothing about what was waiting for them. Born and raised in Utah, Vierig had, at the age of 17, made for Texas with a friend to ride bulls professionally. At 25 years old, after breaking his leg twice as well as an arm and shattering an ankle, he promised himself he wasn't going to end up a beat-up, broken-down cowboy. Instead, he enlisted in the Marines. In some ways it wasn't much of a leap. The daredevil drive that pulsed behind the thrill he got from working the rodeo was the thing that drove him to volunteer for a combat tour. A combat mind-set came to him naturally, and even though no one in-country seemed to know what to do with Vierig or his dog, he put himself to work.

In between missions, Vierig trained Duc on whatever they could find, hiding old mortars and rocket-propelled grenades (RPGs) so the dog could learn the scent. At first Vierig had to ask for missions in order to prove that he and Duc could be useful. He would approach company commanders and battalion commanders and say, "My dog finds bombs. Put us out in front."

After a short time, the SF teams started to request Vierig and Duc. In fact, they all wanted Duc out with them on their missions. Sometime in the spring, after he and Duc had been in-country for a few months, Vierig overheard one of the other Marines say that it'd be more demoralizing for them if Duc were to be killed than if they lost another Marine. He didn't really know until he heard that remark just how much the other guys were depending on the skill of his dog.

Their reputation spread further, beyond their fellow Marines and beyond their base. Whenever he worked with the Iraqi border police, Vierig showed them just how well his dog could find explosives. "Go ahead," he'd say to them. "Hide it. Anywhere you want. My dog will find it." The Iraqi police officers would take a nonexplosive piece of material and tuck it away somewhere. Minutes later Duc would find it. Soon enough, while they were on patrol in the streets, Iraqi civilians would point at the dog and say to Vierig, "Duc?" They knew the dog's name.

Vierig and Duc were stationed in Husaybah, an Iraqi border town known for its lawlessness. The city of about 30,000 people was so treacherous that even Saddam Hussein hadn't been able to keep control over it. It was a dangerous, violent, and volatile place located right on the Syrian border and along the western side of the Euphrates River. The Marines there were constantly engaged in firefights with the insurgents (people in revolt against established authority). They practically had the routine down pat. After an exchange of gunfire, the Marines would give chase down the streets, running past shops and houses. Then the insurgents would rush into a mosque, knowing the Marines would not follow them inside. It was a religious place, a sacred space, and, therefore, off limits. So, the Marines had no choice but to wait. Sometimes the insurgents would emerge and the fighting would begin again. Other times they'd stay inside and the Marines would disengage, knowing that the firefight would pick up again another day.

The insurgents would leave threatening notes for the Marines on the doors of the mosque. One day a note, partly in Arabic and partly in English, caught Vierig's eye. It had the standard threats promising to decapitate Americans and cook their brains. But then he saw the word "Duck." It was spelled like the waterfowl, but the bounty it promised was for a hit on his dog. Next to it was a number: 10,000. Whether it was the guarantee of dollars or some other currency, Vierig wasn't sure, but he knew the enemy was gunning for his dog. And that was when he really realized the impact he and Duc were making.

5

When he first arrived in Iraq, Lulofs was a fairly religious man. Being someone who also put a lot of stock in quiet humility, at first he just couldn't contend with Farnsworth's foul mouth and lewd jokes. They were the only two canine handlers stationed at Camp Baharia, and while the men didn't butt heads exactly, they spent their first weeks together in an uncomfortable quiet. But eventually a grudging respect grew between them. Lulofs could see that behind all the boasting, Farnsworth was a competent handler. Lulofs liked the way the guy worked his dog, Eesau. And sharing such close living quarters, he would sometimes overhear Farnsworth speaking to his wife back home. Somewhere along the way the distance between the men closed, and soon the handlers and their dogs became a tight-knit unit of four.

From day to day, their job was mostly running traffic control points in different locations along the main routes in and out of Fallujah. Lulofs and Farnsworth eventually got their own Humvee from two Marine handlers so they could travel with their dogs. It was a Frankenstein hybrid, a blend of ill-fitting pieces, part pickup truck, part jeep, part tractor. After a couple of months, it took on the look of a hardened scab. It was dinged, dented, scorched, and bruised.

When Lulofs and Farnsworth started taking the vehicle on missions, making the trip between Camp Baharia and Fallujah, the Humvee didn't have any armor, nothing, not even a bulletproof windshield. They were given a couple of Kevlar blankets, which couldn't have stopped a bullet or warded off shrapnel. Still, it was all they had, so they draped the blankets along the carriage in the back where they kept the dog kennels. Bit by bit they clamped on additions to their Humvee, stitching together mismatched patches of metal and canvas. They added L-shaped armored doors for the driver and passenger side and a homemade air-conditioning unit they jerry-rigged to a generator and lobbed onto the roof. It was an eyesore of a combat vehicle, one that stood out in any convoy, and it became a prime and sought-after target.

It didn't take long before there was a bounty on the four of them. Shortly after the first handler-dog teams arrived in 2004, the going rate for taking them out was $10,000. Lulofs was determined to mess up the enemy so much that by the time they left Iraq, the bounty would be at least $25,000.

Early one day in August, they were riding in a convoy on their way to set up a traffic control point. There were very few cars on Main Supply Route Mobile that morning. Lulofs felt that something was off as soon as they rolled out onto the paved thoroughfare. It was too quiet. The six-lane highway usually had more traffic this time of day. They guessed that word of some impending threat had spread among the people living in the city, causing civilians to avoid their normal route and use the makeshift dirt road that ran alongside Main Supply Route Mobile instead.

After some back-and-forth on their radios, Lulofs, Farnsworth, and the Marines in their convoy determined that they were most likely looking at a single IED attack. So they slowed down their normal speed of 45 miles per hour to about 25 and took it nice and easy. Lulofs drove, keeping his eyes locked on the road, looking for a suspicious bump, a rock pile, anything that could be a bomb.

The convoy crept along for some time. Suddenly there was an explosion. It was an IED, but it was also a signal to the enemy, who had been lying in wait, that the convoy was now in sight. The insurgents began to unload their arsenal. Their onslaught hit the convoy from the left side. While Lulofs drove, focused on steering around any IEDs, he also aimed his weapon out the window, shooting as he went. Farnsworth, who didn't have a clear shot from the passenger's seat, kept his eyes glued in front. He watched for danger, called out directions, and reloaded Lulofs's weapon. All the while, incoming fire pelted the convoy of trucks as they pressed forward like ants in a line unable to scatter.

One of the rounds hit Lulofs and Farnsworth's Humvee. A bullet pierced its armor and passed right between Lulofs's knees. It struck the steering wheel column and then ricocheted up and exploded the dashboard. Little blackened bits of shrapnel sprayed everywhere, breaking the skin along Lulofs's hands, legs, chest, and arms.

Lulofs barely had time to react when Farnsworth shouted, "RPG!" Lulofs flinched and slammed on the brakes, keeping the RPG from hitting the driver's side door. The barrage continued. Farnsworth climbed out his side of the moving vehicle to position himself so he could return fire over the back end of the truck.

The guys in the vehicle behind watched as Lulofs and Farnsworth's Humvee got slammed. They counted at least six RPGs that sailed past or hit the vehicle without detonating. Each RPG that hit clanked against the armor at an angle and flew back into the air. It was a relentless hail of bullets and mortars that lasted the full stretch of a mile.

When they finally were able to pull over, the first thing Lulofs and Farnsworth did was check on their dogs. Aaslan had weathered the barrage okay. Eesau had not. He refused to come out of his kennel. Even after Farnsworth finally managed to coax him out, Eesau still wouldn't work. The stress was so great, the dog had just shut down.

The dogs had had some protection against bullets, but it had been modest at best. As each round had hit the side of the vehicle close to the dogs, Lulofs figured they'd been wounded or even killed. It was amazing that they didn't have a scratch on them. But they had come close. On the outside of the vehicle, right by the dogs' kennels, was a compartment where they kept their prepackaged field rations. Later, when they opened one, they found a bullet lodged inside.

6

After that ambush, Lulofs began to change. He'd been deployed for nearly six months, and the devout man he'd been when he arrived in Iraq now saw things differently. Where before he shook his head at the sound of swearing, profanity now spouted freely from his own mouth. Farnsworth noticed the difference in his friend and tried to talk to Lulofs about it. He reasoned that if a guy who wouldn't even utter a curse word put his Bible in a bag and never touched it again, something wasn't right.

When they went out on missions, Lulofs stopped carrying his rifle. He only took his sidearm. He started to think he was invincible. He believed that bullets and bombs couldn't touch him, since he'd already faced so many and survived. God wasn't going to let him die, not here. Not in Fallujah.

The nearer he came to the end of his deployment, the more the thought of going home began to consume Lulofs. He began to approach each mission with a ravenous sense of purpose, working his handlers and their dogs to the breaking point. On one mission during those last weeks, he worked his team so hard that he didn't even realize they had pushed their way past the front line. He had put his dog teams between the Marines and the enemy. When he finally noticed they were in the kill zone, Lulofs simply told his handlers to keep moving even as they were getting shot at. He told them to ignore it. They were less than 100 yards from where artillery shells were landing. He knew how dangerous it was, but he didn't seem to care.

Lulofs rationalized away the risks he was taking. The sooner they were done with this mission, the sooner they could begin the next, and then, only then, could they leave this god-forsaken place and go home.

The sense of fearlessness and invincibility he felt on missions was, Lulofs would realize later, purely selfish. It put him and others recklessly close to the edge of death. Looking back now, Lulofs believes he survived the war because of two things. One of those things was luck. The other was Aaslan. The dog was his one emotional crutch and the reason why he'd been able to hold on to as much of himself as he could in Fallujah.

The other men relied on Aaslan too. During their deployment, Lulofs had one rule about his dog. No one could pet Aaslan while they were working. The Marines on their patrols knew and respected this rule. They would wait for each mission to be over because that's when Aaslan was free to be loved on and to play.

There were a lot of bad days in Iraq, "bad" meaning that there were severe casualties. After one very bad day, Lulofs and

IN THE LINE OF FIRE   21

Aaslan were waiting with the Marines to remount so they could
get back to their base. Lulofs watched one Marine break down,
put his head on Aaslan's shoulder, and weep.

7

It was raining, or at least it had been. The morning ground
was wet and muddy. It was spring 2010, the rainy season
in Kandahar Province, Afghanistan, and Staff Sergeant Justin
Kitts was up early. He washed his face and brushed his teeth
using bottled water, because there was no plumbing or electricity. The base, Strong Point Haji Rahmuddin, was small and
remote. Outside the makeshift gate and beyond the safety of
the military-constructed border were open farmland and grape
fields.

The day's mission was pretty standard. Kitts's unit had
orders to travel to a nearby town and meet with a few of the
locals. Every now and then, as part of its efforts to build better
relationships with the people of Afghanistan, the Army sent in
soldiers to see if the locals needed anything. The soldiers packed
their pockets with candy to hand out to the children who lived
there. But they were also hoping to find people who could become reliable and friendly sources of information about the
Taliban, people who would gather new intelligence and report
any suspicious activity in the area.

Along with 20 other members of the 101st Airborne and
an Afghan interpreter, Kitts geared up and prepared his detection dog, Dyngo, to accompany them. To keep from being easy
to track, the unit avoided the hardened surface road, which was

a shorter, more direct route. Instead, they walked through a grape field, its earthen-packed walls each about waist high and covered in tangled vines. Hopping over them slowed down the patrol but made their movements less obvious.

The gray weather started to clear as they walked through the field. The sun came out and then, suddenly, so did the sound of gunfire. It was an ambush. Kitts, Dyngo, and the rest of the unit ran for the cover of some higher walls that flanked the main road, the sound of boots pounding the ground. Once they reached the road, the soldiers spread out along the front wall and took aim with their guns, while a few others stayed behind them, covering the wall on the other side of the grape field and laying down suppressive fire.

The unit called for air support, but they knew it would take a while to arrive. In the meantime, they would have to hold their ground yet also find a way to move out of their vulnerable position.

Kitts took Dyngo to look for an exit route. He started down the road to the left, sending Dyngo up ahead. He watched the dog carefully put his nose to the ground. When Dyngo was about 100 feet out, Kitts noticed a change in the dog's search pattern. Dyngo began taking in deep, sweeping breaths. He knew something was there. Kitts shouted to Dyngo, calling him back.

The others in the unit pulled back from the left side of the road. But they were still trying to return gunfire at an enemy they could not track or see. Kitts pulled Dyngo down against the walls, keeping the dog low and close to him for cover. Suddenly the enemy shot two RPGs toward them. The first went over the back wall and exploded in the field behind them. But the second flew into the wall and destoyed a chunk of it just 10 feet from where they sat.

The explosion registered with a deep shock to the ground and a deafening noise. Dyngo began to whimper. It was a high whining sound the seven-year-old Belgian Malinois rarely made. Kitts knew his dog was not simply reacting to the noise or the chaos. The pressure from the RPG blast and the shock wave were causing real pain to Dyngo's sensitive ears. Dyngo collapsed on his stomach. His limbs went limp, and his ears flattened. The dog was afraid.

Kitts instinctively broke off a branch from a nearby tree and pushed the branch under Dyngo's nose. The dog latched onto it and began a nervous, mindless gnawing, the canine version of hand-wringing. Kitts pulled on the branch and they played a little game of tug-of-war.

Dyngo was usually so calm, unshakable. Even when they took helicopter rides, as they frequently did, Dyngo never minded the noise. Unlike some of the other MWDs, who were easily frightened by a chopper's noise or balked at the strong, rough winds kicked out from its fast-beating blades, Dyngo always hopped on happily and pushed his muzzle as close to the window as he could so he could see what was happening on the ground. To see him unhinged, to see this normally calm and experienced dog so stressed, filled Kitts with dread. But soon the release of energy from playing with the branch calmed Dyngo and also settled Kitts's own rising nerves.

The incoming gunfire was still distant and intermittent, so the leader of their unit asked Kitts to clear the right side of the road, hoping that this could help them work their way farther from the ambush in that direction. Despite being shaken, Dyngo followed Kitts's instruction to "seek." He trotted along, working quickly, sniffing over patches of dirt, over clusters and clumps of road and grass. When Kitts saw Dyngo slow, once again growing more intense, more deliberate, the handler called the dog back even before he had time to give the final alert. Kitts didn't need to see it. There was no doubt that Dyngo was on bomb for a second time. Now the unit couldn't move left or right. They were trapped on the road. The only way out was back through the grape field.

It seemed like forever, but it was only a few more minutes before the air support arrived. Shortly after that, there was no more enemy fire. The grape field went quiet. The enemy had retreated. It was now safe for the soldiers to retrace their steps.

An EOD team arrived to remove the bombs. Buried nearly two feet deep in the ground were two yellow jugs, each packed with 50 pounds of explosives. They had cunningly been hidden only about 200 yards apart. The Taliban had deliberately flushed the soldiers out of the grape field and onto the road, where their path was boxed in on both sides by IEDs. Everyone in that patrol had been in the kill zone—not once but twice.

If it had not been for Dyngo, they might all be dead.

8

Today little flecks of white color Dyngo's muzzle just below his nose, as if he's just lifted his head from sniffing powdery snow. His soft amber eyes have a tired, well-worn quality, but they still brighten with interest when someone he likes walks into a room or, especially, when it's time to work. He has a stout and sturdy body and large head with an expressive face. Dyngo is a dog who smiles.

As a younger dog, Dyngo had a reputation for being a little hellion and something of a biter. But he is beginning to slow down. He's changed over the last year. Two back-to-back deployments have taken their toll. Even though you can see that his body aches, the dog still loves to work and works to please.

Over their six-and-a-half-month deployment, Dyngo accompanied Kitts on 63 missions. And during all those missions, Kitts only fired his weapon twice. Once was that day in the grape field. The other time was during a routine patrol, and it was to protect Dyngo. Kitts had seen a yard dog out of the corner of his eye. The dog, mangy and gaunt, his hackles bristling, had caught wind of Dyngo. The closer they got, the deeper and more threatening the yard dog's barking became. He wore

Tech Sergeant Justin Kitts and his MWD partner Dyngo take a break in the shade while they compete in the K-9 trials hosted at Lackland Air Force Base in Texas in May 2012.

a metal chain around his neck, but Kitts could see that it was broken and that nothing was keeping him tied down. When the yard dog charged at Dyngo, Kitts raised his nine-millimeter handgun and fired, killing the other dog instantly.

There is a closeness between Dyngo and Kitts that has remained intact, even after Dyngo was paired up with another handler. Despite spending six months apart, Dyngo still tunes in to Kitts's every movement. His eyes and nose follow Kitts like the point of a compass always bobbing to north. After his deployment, Kitts became a tech sergeant and an instructor at YPG. He taught other handlers on their way to war, sharing his experiences.

Like so many other handlers who have bonded with the dogs they deployed with, Kitts wanted to adopt Dyngo. He felt a sense of ownership and believed he was the best one to take care of the dog after he retired, just as he had cared for Dyngo after that day in the grape field in Afghanistan. When they'd finally made it back to their patrol base after the ambush, Dyngo was exhausted and nervous. The dog went for days without eating. He was heavy-lidded and melancholy. Kitts was patient. He gave Dyngo room to recover and refused to work him until the dog was rested. In just a few days, Dyngo came around and started to act like his old self.

Even though they were now both stateside, Kitts was going to have to wait for the chance to adopt his former partner. It would be at least another seven months, or however long the dog's next deployment would take. Dyngo already had orders to go back to Afghanistan and back to war.

9

Any handler who has brought a dog with him to war will say it made all the difference in the world. He will say that having the dog by his side provided him more than just a living, breathing piece of home. The dog was a talisman, a powerful charm that insulated the handler from whatever horrors unfolded, bringing him peace in turbulence and offering companionship in times of loneliness. The dog's presence made the path through war bearable.

No matter how far a handler strays from working with dogs, either within the military or back in civilian life, K-9 is a lifelong state of mind. It's like a bloodline, deep and tangled, the mark of which lives on long past the dogs, long after the wars are over.

Ron Aiello, a dog handler who served in Vietnam, is a case in point. Aiello still beams with pride for the dog who accompanied him to war. From the vivid and joyful way Aiello talks about her, it's as if Stormy is somehow still at his feet or dozing in the next room, instead of a memory nearly half a century old. She did more, Aiello believes, than merely save the lives of men on the patrols he led through the jungles of Vietnam, alerting them to snipers, ambushes, and explosives. Had it not been for Stormy, he said, "I would've come back a different person."

Even when Aiello was a little boy, he knew he would someday become a Marine. He grew up in his grandparents' home in

Trenton, New Jersey, in a house filled with love, food, dogs, and family. One of Aiello's favorite uncles was a Marine. So, in the summer of 1964, when he was 18, Aiello enlisted. A few weeks later, he was an infantry grunt stationed at Camp Lejeune in North Carolina. One day coming back from maneuvers, Aiello saw a notice on a bulletin board asking for volunteers for dog school. Aiello thought, if he had to go to Vietnam, what better way to do it than with a dog?

By December 1965, Aiello was assigned to and training with the Army's dog program at Fort Benning in Georgia. It was there Aiello met Stormy, an 18-month-old German shepherd mix. Day after day they trained together on day patrols and then night patrols. With Aiello, Stormy learned to become a scout dog. She learned how to follow airborne scents and alert on booby traps, the smell of gun oil, and the sound of snipers high in the trees. The training drew them close, and pretty soon Aiello felt like Stormy could read his mind. In 1966, the 21-year-old Marine corporal and his dog were on their way to Vietnam.

As a scout dog team, their role was to lead night patrols through the jungle undetected and in one piece. Aiello always kept Stormy's leash wrapped tightly around his left wrist. Stormy, confident in her job, would lead out in front. When the leash was taut and pulling, the tension held between them, she was moving and it was safe to follow. But as a soon as the leash went slack, it meant Stormy had stopped. This was her way of alerting Aiello, who would then halt the troops behind them. Whatever held Stormy's attention, whichever direction her head was turned, that was where the threat could be found.

Before each mission, Aiello sat with Stormy and talked through his orders with her. "Stormy," he'd say, bending down to the dog, "we're going out on a patrol tonight. We're gonna go to an old cemetery." As he talked, mapping out the mission klick by klick, Stormy sat, studied his face, and listened intently. Aiello would look at Stormy and tell her when it was time to go. He would feel worry-free at this point, all because Stormy had been there to listen.

Stormy was a lovable, friendly dog. In fact, she was so friendly that when a senior officer ordered Aiello to use Stormy to intimidate a member of the Vietcong they were holding captive for questioning, Aiello panicked. Stormy was too gentle a dog to be violent without provocation, without some kind of imminent threat. As Aiello approached the man, who was on his knees, blindfolded, with hands tied behind his back, he tightened his grip on Stormy's leash. He was not afraid that she would bite the prisoner but rather that, if she got too close, she would lick his face.

That sweet disposition could change, however, if the situation warranted it. One afternoon on base, Aiello and Stormy were crossing a field. Tired and deep in thought, Aiello didn't notice a South Vietnamese Army soldier who was also crossing the field and heading right toward him. The soldier was similarly unaware of Aiello and his dog. Stormy, however, had seen this man coming at them and, perhaps because she didn't know him or because she smelled his gun, she marked him as a threat. She stopped in front of Aiello, crouched to the ground, and growled. The soldier, reacting, pointed his gun at the dog. Aiello reached for his .45-caliber pistol and pointed it at the man's head. He had no idea if the Vietnamese soldier would understand him, but he told him anyway, "If you try to shoot my dog, I will blow your head off." The soldier lowered his weapon and very slowly backed away. Aiello lowered his weapon and then, sensing that someone was close by, turned around. Behind him

were three other Marines who'd watched the Vietnamese soldier point his gun at Stormy. They had their M14 rifles raised,
ready to shoot him or anyone else who tried to harm her.

10

After one handler was shot and wounded, Aiello and
Stormy took over his assignment for a day patrol. Their
orders were to search a village suspected of harboring Vietcong. However, before they began their search, an air strike
came through. Artillery hailed down in front of them, and the
roars of jets filled the air above them. The ground shook as
500-pound bombs hit the village and rattled the earth.

Aiello stood on a hillside and watched as the village
turned into a fiery inferno. While he and the others waited for
it to cool, a sick feeling filled Aiello. He knew they weren't prepared for what lay ahead. Aiello was drenched with sweat from
the intense heat of all that burning, and from the mere sight of
it. The trees were still scorching hot, the lush green leaves smol-
dering and smoking. Like lit coals, their ashes lifted up into the
mess of black clouds above them even as the soldiers made their
way to the bottom of the hill.

When they entered the village, Stormy made a sound
Aiello had never heard before. It was a deep, strangled moan.
As they pushed deeper into the wreckage, she kept moaning.
Stormy had been trained not just to alert on ammunition and
gun oil but also on human scent. She was overwhelmed by the
smell of charred flesh. It was all around them. Aiello realized
there was no way she could work like this. But in the end it

didn't matter. As they walked, Aiello couldn't understand what they were doing there. There was nothing left to find but bodies. Pieces and parts were strewn everywhere. The village was like a furnace, the temperature upward of 120 degrees.

The memory of that day was one that Aiello repressed. It hid in the recesses of his mind until it reemerged on a steamy summer night over 30 years later.

On July 4, 2000, late in the evening, Aiello was sitting on the porch of his New Jersey home. Earlier, his teenage sons had set off Roman candles and firecrackers in the yard. Maybe it was the sound of the fireworks, or the starbursts pluming in the distant sky, or even the hazy heat of the night, but the vision hit him suddenly and clearly, as did the sensation of being completely soaked. He flashed back to his younger self, standing at the top of that hill in 1966, surveying the burning wreckage of that Vietnamese village.

11

Perhaps even more traumatizing than the memory of that day in the charred Vietnamese village is that Aiello never knew what became of Stormy. When his tour in Vietnam was over in 1967, Stormy stayed behind, as each dog did when his handler finished a tour. Back then, the dogs stayed where they were and partnered up with new handlers.

Aiello remembers the April afternoon when his captain announced that the replacement handlers would be arriving the next day. It was, he told them, the last night they would have with their dogs. Almost all of the handlers, including Aiello, brought blankets out to the kennels to sleep on the ground next to their dogs. They wanted to be with them until the very last moment.

For years afterward, Aiello wrote to the Marine Corps again and again, trying to find Stormy, putting in his bid to take her. He mailed letters and made phone calls, but to no avail. He never received a response and was left completely in the dark about what had become of her.

Marine handler Ron Aiello and his scout dog Stormy deployed to Vietnam together in 1966. Aiello, whose tour ended in 1967, never knew what became of his canine partner.

Credit: Courtesy of Ron Aiello

Some 10,000 dog handlers served in the Vietnam War. The majority never saw their dogs again. Nearly 5,000 dogs served in Vietnam from 1964 to 1975. Of those, only 204 dogs left the country. None was outprocessed to life beyond the military. The dogs in-country at the time the US forces evacuated were either euthanized or turned over to the South Vietnamese Army, which most likely meant they were killed and perhaps even eaten. Vietnam is just one of several countries where it is acceptable to eat dog meat.

In the early 1990s, Aiello and some of his Vietnam handler buddies saw a notice about a war dog reunion in Ocean City, Maryland. They decided to go. They didn't realize until they got to the hotel that it was actually a reunion for World War II handlers. In the end, Aiello said it didn't matter—the difference in wars or the generations between them—they were all handlers.

Aiello and the other Vietnam veterans spent three days laughing, talking, and sharing memories of their dogs with the World War II veterans. "They would close their eyes and listen," he said. "Their stories were our stories."

part two

training for war

*The guard dog was incorruptible; the police dog depend-
able; the messenger dog reliable. The human watchman
might be bought; not so the dog. The soldier sentinel might
fall asleep; never the dog. The battlefield runner might
fail . . . but the dog, to his last breath would follow the
line of duty.*

—Ernest Harold Baynes,
Animal Heroes of the Great War

12

Taint, one of the dogs at the Lackland Air Force Base kennels in 1999, was an ornery, raging beast of a dog. He was a notorious biter who had grown to deserve his name. Dr. Stewart Hilliard, chief of the MWD training course at the Department of Defense (DOD) and resident animal behaviorist, asked handler Staff Sergeant Chris Jakubin to work with him to test Taint's boundaries. They would see if Taint could still work in the program.

Jakubin was eager to help. He had a great respect for Hilliard, whom he called Doc, and often trailed around after him, peppering Doc with questions about training techniques or a dog he was having trouble with.

Before Jakubin entered Taint's kennel the first time, he donned the necessary protective layers and pulled on a pair of gloves to shield his hands. They were expecting the worst.

But when Jakubin opened the door to go in, nothing happened. He offered Taint a hot dog, which the dog accepted. Taint let Jakubin walk right in. Jakubin didn't have any issues with Taint that day or in the days that followed. He would just walk up to the kennel, feed Taint a hot dog, and go on in. On the way out, the dog followed him willingly. And that is how Taint the problem dog became Jakubin's dog.

Jakubin's assignment at Lackland in San Antonio, Texas, eventually came to an end, and a Marine took over handling Taint. Jakubin was very clear about how to work with the dog to keep his temperament in check. He had carefully outlined a long list of dos and don'ts. The Marine assured him he could manage Taint. But one day, not long after Jakubin had left, the Marine tried to get too close. Taint mauled him so badly that Lackland's behavioral veterinarians were ready to destroy the dog. When Jakubin heard this, he pleaded with them not to put the dog down. "I will take him," he told them. "I will deal with him."

His request was approved, and Taint was flown to Colorado Springs, Colorado, where Jakubin had become kennel master at the US Air Force (USAF) Academy at Fort Carson. It had been months since Jakubin had last seen his old partner, and when he went to pick Taint up, Jakubin was nervous. What if the dog's attitude toward him had changed? So he put on gloves before opening Taint's crate, just in case. But Taint came out of his crate happy to see Jakubin. Together, the two went on to win multiple competitions, and Taint met the requirements for detection work without difficulty.

Fast forward to 2009. Taint turned 10 years old. His health had deteriorated. His bladder was shot, and his cataracts were so bad he was nearly blind. But the tenacious Belgian Malinois continued running drills, and his accuracy at detection remained spot-on perfect. Even though his body was riddled with illness and infirmity, he outperformed dogs half his age and with twice his strength. Those who knew and watched Taint and Jakubin together as a team believed the dog's iron will to survive came solely from his attachment to Jakubin.

One day, during a routine veterinary examination, the vet discovered that Taint's lungs were filling with fluid. It was unlikely, the vet told Jakubin, that Taint would survive the night. So Jakubin took Taint outside. They walked for nearly two miles before he took the dog back to the vet and said good-bye.

Jakubin returned to the kennels alone. It was the first time any of his handlers saw him so emotionally bare. It was the first time they ever saw Jakubin cry.

As is the custom with military kennels, Taint was given a memorial service. When Sergeant Timothy Bailey, Jakubin's head trainer, spoke to the sizable crowd in attendance, he tried to impart to those gathered how rare Jakubin's connection with Taint really had been. Their relationship had spanned most of the dog's life. "Jak and Taint could probably almost go in for records of being the longest team together," he said. "Your average K-9 military dog team is together for maybe three to four years, and that's the max."

Jakubin and Taint had been together for 10.

13

Mack's muzzle was already speckled with gray and white, even though he was barely five years old. It was why the handlers at the USAF Academy called the medium-size Belgian Malinois the ghost-faced killer.

Mack was riding in the back of one of the kennel's vehicles outfitted especially for dogs. Jakubin was driving. Jakubin and Mack were on their way from the USAF Academy in Colorado Springs to meet handlers stationed at Buckley, an Air Force base in Aurora, Colorado, for a day of intrabase kennel training.

Mack didn't sit quietly, nor did he use the hour of downtime in the moving car to rest. He was constantly twisting and shifting or scratching at the metal interior of the made-for-canine backseat. He barked randomly at cars that sped by his window on the highway. The bark was throaty, hoarse, and loud. A smoker's bark, Jakubin called it, with a grin. Jakubin had taken a special shine to Mack, the dog he fondly called the reincarnation of Taint.

In the backseat, Mack seemed more stir-crazy than vicious. But Mack hadn't been an easy dog to work with. In that way, Mack was continuing Taint's legacy. He was a challenge. And Jakubin loved a good challenge, especially when it came to training dogs.

A long line of problem dogs graced the kennels under Jakubin's command. In fact, he actively sought out difficult dogs from other kennels. It became something of a tradition,

Chris Jakubin, kennel master of the USAF Academy, and MWD Oli at a training facility in Colorado Springs, Colorado in December 2011.

one that began with the very first dog to officially join the USAF Academy kennels after they first opened in 2002. Agbhar, a German shepherd, did not like people. Agbhar was not friendly. Agbhar was a problem dog.

"Agbhar was in a way a misfit dog. Taint was a misfit dog," Jakubin said. "Like the home for misfit toys, we're the home for misfit dogs."

The kennel master is the officer responsible for maintaining the kennels and overseeing the handlers and dogs who work there. It's a high-ranking position in the dog-handling field. It's also a role that comes with a lot of managerial responsibilities, from ordering the dogs' food to assigning handlers to base patrol duty. Much of the work can have little to do with hands-on training. How much a kennel master works with the dogs is entirely up to him. Will he be a desk man or a dog man?

Jakubin was and still is decidedly a dog man, one who operates under the philosophy that there is no single, cookie-cutter way to train a dog. Each dog is unique, and it's the handler's job to study that dog and learn *that* dog's behavior. As Jakubin sees it, dogs tell their handlers how they need to be trained, not the other way around. All the handlers have to do is listen.

His technique, which he honed while working with dogs like Taint, Agbhar, and Mack, begins with simple observation. First, uncover each dog's weak points and fully explore and understand them. Next, work through those weak points. Finally, build the dog's confidence until that dog is performing at his highest potential. It is a long investigative process but one that comes with great reward. You wind up with a dog who can contribute, a dog who can save lives.

Jakubin has been training dogs for about 30 years, almost his whole adult life. Getting on with dogs comes naturally to him. It all goes back to his first dog bite. One day in winter when he was just a kid, the family dog, a springer spaniel named Silly, went missing. They found the dog a couple of days later at a neighbor's house. When Jakubin went to retrieve Silly, the neighbor's boxer bit him hard. The dog's incisors punctured his leg. Rather than scaring him off dogs for good, though, the experience fortified Jakubin's desire to work with them. He calls it his Peter Parker moment. That was a long time ago, and now Jakubin's arms and legs are pocked and colored with dog-bite scars.

The USAF Academy kennels are set back away from the road on the widespread campus, nestled against the outline of Colorado's mountains. Two mesh-wire sculptures contoured in the shape of dogs guard the front door, flanking the walkway. A worn, black leather couch takes up room in the hallway, the walls of which are lined with framed photographs of each dog who has called this kennel home.

Underneath each photo is a wooden plaque that lists the dog's individual achievements. There's Taint's drug find in May 2003 (five grams of marijuana). There's Ginger's 115 individual bomb searches in August 2003 alone. And there's Agbhar's second-place finish in bomb detection at the Tucson K-9 trials in 2003. This wall of colorful photos and the modest, fenced-in training yard out back, with its seesaw plank of wood and cement tunnel, are reminiscent of a nursery school playground.

Just to the left is the door leading to the kennels themselves, and before that is a clean and organized kitchen area. At the other end of the hall, Jakubin's office is comfortable but cluttered. His desk is a mess of papers. Equipment and gear are lumped in piles on the floor. Shelves and file cabinets are crowded with awards etched with achievements Jakubin never mentioned.

Across the hall, in what appears to be a little-used conference room, an old-fashioned mantelpiece hangs on the wall. A row of decorative tin boxes sits on it. Their sweetly curled pastel ribbons belie their contents. Inside each one are the ashes of a dog the kennel has lost to illness or old age.

When Jakubin first became kennel master at the USAF Academy, the dog program there was so new they didn't even have a kennel, so he and his handlers operated out of an old house on a remote part of the academy's campus. The house is gone now. The area where it once stood is the site of a canine memorial. It's on the top of a little hill. A large, fallen tree with gnarly limbs forms a barrier that closes off the memorial, serving as a fitting, somber fence.

There's a small marker for each dog, a piece of stone that bears a bronze plaque with the dog's likeness etched in black. Ginger's memorial marker is on the exact spot where the old kitchen was and where she used to sleep.

Even after a long career, losing a dog never gets easier. "That's the worst part of the job," Jakubin said. "To see a dog go. I've probably become numb to it over these years, and I still find myself thinking about the dog and shedding a tear."

One afternoon during my visit to the USAF Academy in Colorado, we walked across the campus. Jakubin ran into one of his handlers who had Benga, a German shepherd, in tow. The dog had banged his head, which had caused a hematoma, a mass of blood, to develop on his ear. It was the third mass there. Now his left ear drooped, maybe from the weight of the stitches but more likely, said the vet, as a lasting result of repeated injuries. That ear would probably never stand up straight again.

When Benga saw Jakubin, he immediately lit up with excitement. The dog wanted to get to him. His ears snapped as high and tall as they could go. His eyes widened and a high-pitched whine caught in his throat as he tap-danced his paws up and down, desperate to be closer.

14

When Lackland hosted the interservice Iron Dog Competition in May 2012, I joined Jakubin, who had brought along Mack and some of his handlers from the USAF Academy kennels. Over the course of two days, the competition tested a variety of skills at the core of a handler and dog's education as a team. The course stretched across many miles and was meant to challenge the handler and the dog both physically and mentally. It included a low river crossing, an activity challenge where handlers had to carry their dogs up and down a hill, and a basic obstacle course that included an injured soldier (a heavy dummy that handlers had to carry or drag to safety while still managing their dogs and their weapons).

In addition to the competition, there were a series of classroom seminars and a host of hands-on courses. During his seminar, Jakubin showed the assembled handlers a video of a dog being tested to gauge his reaction to an aggressor. In the video, the handlers conducted a routine traffic stop. Jakubin, in the role of the aggressor, was outfitted all in black. He wore a ski mask and carried a big, black, rubber baton. Jakubin advanced on the dog. At first, the dog tried to defend himself. He started forward toward Jakubin, but then he retreated, skirting backward, trying to hide behind his handler. Jakubin backed off. He took a few steps away and lowered his weapon.

After a few minutes, he gave the dog another chance to engage and defend himself by advancing on both the handler and the dog with his voice raised. But again the dog showed a clear lack of confidence. He gave a few short barks, but ultimately he retreated. Jakubin pulled off the ski mask. He didn't need to be tough on the dog or try again. He knew the dog was done.

When the video ended, Jakubin explained to the seminar attendees that what they had just seen was a dog who didn't have the right kind of fight to be a patrol dog. But, he said, that's okay. Not all dogs are meant to be patrol dogs. And that is no reflection on a handler's abilities. Just because the dog failed the test, it didn't mean the handler did.

During another training seminar, this one held at Langley Air Force Base in Newport News, Virginia, in 2011, I had watched Jakubin coach a handler working on a drill with her dog. Most of the other handlers had finished for the day, but this one continued to struggle with the task in front of her. She tried to focus on each tip Jakubin gave her, her face crinkled in concentration. Later that day when the seminar ended, Jakubin was impressed. He said that what the handler lacked in skill, she more than made up for in persistence. In this profession, the handler's drive to learn is just as crucial as the dog's, perhaps even more so.

15

Canine training can be a rough-and-tumble business. It takes a toll on the body. The resulting scratches, knuckle nicks, and bite marks, like scorecards, are brands of the job and worn with pride. The badder the dog, the bigger the bite. The deeper the scar, the better the story.

On a training field, one young handler pulled off his shirt and upended his bandages to reveal the bite he had received the day before. In this case, the dog hadn't taken a temperamental turn. Rather, it was the handler who had made a move in the wrong direction during their bite-work training. The dog, aiming for the protective layers, missed and ended up raking off a good bit of skin right under the handler's rib cage. Because the dog's teeth only grazed the handler's side, the marks looked more like angry red scratches that were deeper where the canines had pierced the flesh.

In the PowerPoint presentation Jakubin used during his seminar, one of the slides showed a particularly heinous dog bite inflicted on a handler, Staff Sergeant Ciara Gavin. The label over the photo read "Super Epic Failure!!"

The photo showed that Gavin's skin had been ripped so completely, it looked as though a crude blade had sliced a square patch from the fleshiest section of her forearm. Blood pooled in the wound, threatening to spill over the edge. The rest of her arm was spotted with drops of red. Jakubin was with

Gavin before she was rushed to the hospital. It was the worst dog bite he had ever seen.

Gavin worked in Jakubin's kennel, where initially she had been partnered with a long-haired German shepherd who had a sweet temperament. While that dog had been competent in detection work, he never took to bite work. Jakubin traded him to another base that was having trouble with a dog named Kelly. Kelly was notorious for her volatile temperament and erratic moods. She had bitten at least three handlers and sent them each to the hospital. When she came to the USAF Academy kennels, Kelly was assigned to Gavin. It was Kelly who tore that piece out of Gavin's arm.

Kelly's K-9 portrait hangs in the hallway of the academy's kennel with the others. Her forehead is stout and square, and her ears lean at a somewhat sharper bend, turning out at their own stubborn angle. The lids of her eyes have a reddish hue and actually seem to glow. There is no other way to describe it: The dog looks evil.

At best, Kelly was merely unpredictable. Her moods changed suddenly and without warning or provocation. One minute Kelly would be vicious, and the next she'd be compliant, lying on her back, offering her belly up for a scratch. Gavin would see the flash of evil and then it would disappear again. And when Kelly went to that ferocious place, snarling and bucking, it was like a rodeo. Wrangling her back down into submission was no easy feat.

There was nothing especially foreboding about the day Kelly bit Gavin. She and Jakubin were just trying to work the dog through the fierce possessiveness she showed for her toys. They were attempting to establish Kelly's trust and consistency by showing her that if she released a toy, she would get it back again.

Gavin was standing behind Kelly, raising her arms and lifting the dog by the collar, when Kelly whipped her head around and sank her teeth into Gavin's arm.

It was six weeks before Gavin was able to use her hand again. When she returned to work, Jakubin put Kelly's leash back in Gavin's hand. She took it without thinking twice. Gavin could have refused, but in her mind, picking up Kelly's leash wasn't a choice. Pure pride and ego kept her going. In the end, it was the good kind of ego. It prevented her from letting her fear override her confidence. It's this ego in a canine handler that inspires persistence and the kind of commitment that separates a good handler from a great one. It was essential that Gavin get right back to work and push through her fears of working with Kelly. It made Gavin a better handler.

Kelly eventually went to a different kennel. Gavin completed her career as an Air Force handler in 2008. And though Gavin is no longer an MWD handler, she will never forget that bite. Even from a distance, the twisted lines of the scar shine a pearly white.

Gavin recently saw Kelly. The dog seemed calm and under control. But, for a few seconds, the old devil in Kelly showed through. When the dog growled and snapped at her new handler, adrenaline coursed through Gavin and her heart thundered as if it would never settle back down.

But as they say in K-9, it's not a matter of *if* you'll get bitten, only when.

16

I could feel the soggy Virginia heat on my face, but it was actually cool inside the enormous black bite suit I was wearing. This luxurious damp was, I was fully aware, lingering sweat from the bodies that had worn the suit during drills the day before, but I didn't care. The suit was my big, bulky armor of protection.

Over the loud thumping of my heart, I could hear calls from the small crowd gathered inside the smaller training yard to watch me catch my first bite. "Catching a bite" is essentially the act of becoming the human equivalent of a chew toy. And it's a crucial part of a handler's role in preparing his dog for patrol work.

Bite-work training is learned in stages. This is for everyone's safety—the dog's, the handler's, and the decoy's. The decoy is a handler playing the role of "perpetrator" so the dog can learn how to detain a fleeing suspect during patrol work. If a decoy turns the wrong way or keeps his body too rigid, he can really hurt the dog or himself. The decoy wears a bite sleeve or a full bite suit. Bite suits vary in size and bulk, but their weight is gradually reduced until the decoy is wearing something thin enough to hide under street clothes. This way a dog learns to associate the bite with a perpetrator rather than with the suit.

The first suit I tried on was huge. Two women handlers, the only other women beside myself in this group, helped me into the gear. They held out their arms so I had something to hang on to and worked the zippers running down the side of the pant legs to squash them low to the ground, so that I could climb into them. The jacket was easier to get on but not easy to wear. It was very heavy and very large.

Jakubin stepped in, shook his head, and handed me a tack suit jacket, which was just as big but not as bulky and thick. It didn't fit exactly, but it was close enough. Under the weight of the jacket and the pants, I felt like I was walking neck deep through a pool, pushing against a wall of water. I was expected to act the part of a fleeing suspect and "run" away from a dog. But I could hardly manage a respectable walk.

Handler Staff Sergeant Ted Carlson brought out the dog who was going to bite me, a slender Dutch shepherd named Rambo. From across the yard, I heard Rambo's ragged panting, his high-pitched whining, and the sound of his teeth smacking together as he snapped at the air in anticipation. The sight of me in the suit had ignited his "prey drive," the instinct that motivates a dog to chase and bite something into submission. It seemed that Rambo's prey drive was quite high. My brain knew that I was safe, but my body didn't. My muscles stiffened in a physical, primal, fear response.

Jakubin stood with me in the middle of the yard and adjusted my stance. Before he left me there on my own, he offered one final directive. "If you get knocked down, don't move," he said. "I'll come and pick you up."

I held my breath, shut my eyes, and waited for the blow. It took Rambo under three seconds to clear the 25 feet separating us. I felt a spike of adrenaline as the dog made contact, the force of his weight shoving me back as his open mouth locked around my arm. The sensation registered from dull to crisp, the trickle before the deluge, as I felt teeth sink into me. That sensation was pain.

17

Dogs have 42 teeth, but it is the big fangs, called canines, that are the real damage-doers. Canine teeth are sharp, and they grab onto and puncture flesh. In addition, a dog's straight, muscular jaw is designed for meat eating.

Different studies and tests have been conducted to try to measure bite impact in a variety of species. Per square inch, the human bite exerts 120 pounds of pressure. That's enough to do some damage. Think about Mike Tyson, the boxer who managed to tear away a piece of Evander Holyfield's ear with his teeth. Depending on the breed, dog bites boast much more force. The military most often employs Belgian Malinois and German shepherds. According to the Air Force, the average military working dog's bite exerts somewhere between 400 and 700 pounds of pressure.

In training a dog to attack and detain a suspect, the objective is for him to get a full-mouth bite with a solid grip. The strength of the bite comes from the clamp of the jaws. A weak bite happens when, for example, only a dog's front teeth catch the material. That's not a bite that will hold for long. But the power of a dog bite depends on many things, from the obvious, such as how large the dog is, to the difficult to measure or to predict with regularity, such as the dog's desire to bite.

I can't say for sure exactly how many pounds of pressure came down on my arm. Rambo wasn't a very big dog, and I was fully aware that what I was experiencing was hardly pushing the limits of dog-bite pain. Because I knew this, I gritted my teeth, forced a smile, and took a few steps around the yard. But Rambo had a good, full-mouth bite, and he remained fastened to me. Whenever I moved, I dragged him along. Jakubin encouraged me to try to pull my arm away from the dog. But the resistance excited Rambo. It activated his prey drive, which in turn further ignited his desire to bite. I tugged my arm for all I was worth, but Rambo's grip seemed only to get stronger.

We repeated this move of run, jump, and bite a few more times. When I finally took off the suit, a marking the shape of a dog's open mouth had already puffed pink and purple on my upper right arm, a swollen pinch where the dog's jaw had clamped down on my flesh. Within an hour, that marking billowed into a righteous bruise of deep blues and greens. Compared to some of the batterings I had seen on arms far more muscular and experienced than my own, this mark was like holding up a paper cut next to a machete wound.

That didn't, however, keep me from regarding the bruise fondly over the next couple of weeks, proud as its coloring molted into withering shades of yellow and brown. When Rambo's imprint finally faded and disappeared completely, I was sorry to see it go.

18

I had the leash in my hand. Haus, the handsome German shorthaired pointer on the other end, looked up at me warily. He was not exactly a willing partner. We were standing together at the threshold of a restroom at Buckley Air Force

Base. Hypothetically, there was a bomb in the bathroom, and it was our job to find it.

Haus was an experienced detection and patrol dog who had deployed five times and had a solid record of finds. His body and legs were white and flecked with brown, except for one round patch of brown on his back that looked like a small, high-riding saddle. The color matched his silky ears. I tried to give him a look of reassurance and solidarity, but I must not have pulled it off. Haus threw a glance of concern and confusion in Jakubin's direction and at the rest of the group he knew and trusted who were crowding around the entrance behind us.

I wasn't sure how to begin, so I turned to Tech Sergeant Edward Canell, Buckley's kennel master. "Just clear the room," he said. That was all the help he offered. A host of faces pressed even closer together in the door frame. I was being tested. The fluorescent lights of the bathroom were hospital bright and had the nerve-wracking effect of a big shining spotlight.

The bathroom was hardly large. It had a few empty stalls, a long counter with a few sinks, and a couple of urinals. I was relatively confident I could do this. I had just spent the morning watching a handful of teams search the base chapel and a number of other rooms, sniffing out drugs and explosives.

I pointed my hand down to the seam where the wall met the floor, mimicking the gesture I'd seen handlers use. Miraculously, Haus put his nose to the very spot I had indicated and followed as I led us forward. "Seek," I told him. I meant to give a clear, forceful command, but my voice sounded hollow and small.

Haus and I moved along as best as I could direct him, clearing the counter and sinks. Trouble hit when we got to the bathroom stalls. The dog followed my lead into the first stall and around the basin of the first toilet bowl, but having to hold the door open for both of us tripped me up and he darted ahead of me, skipping a stall. When I pulled him back, the leash got tangled around his legs. I managed to free Haus the first time. The second time, just a minute later, we were a tangled mess. The door of the stall knocked into my back. I was exasperated.

Haus gave up on me right then and there. He sat in the middle of the bathroom and turned expectantly to Jakubin, as if appraising my performance with a look that said "Clearly, you can't be serious."

"Give up?" Canell asked, his eyes twinkling. I gave one last desperate scan around the room but nodded. I could feel the heat rising in my cheeks.

Canell walked me to the paper towel dispenser. It was your standard stainless steel container with brown paper towels. There, as plain as day, was a sizable piece of duct tape, plastered above the keyhole of the clearly broken cabinet. It was out of place against the otherwise well-maintained and clean bathroom. He pulled back the tape and opened the compartment, revealing the "bomb."

In my hurry to perform well, or get away from the crowd of observers, I'd breezed right by this now painfully obvious visual clue. If I had been looking more carefully, it would've been the very first thing I saw coming into the bathroom. But I hadn't been using my eyes. I had been relying on Haus to do the work. I had focused all my attention on him, and my clear inexperience and confusion ran right down the leash to the dog. He knew the moment I gave up even as I was trying to hide it, and he exposed me by sitting in the middle of the room and giving up the search.

It was a fast but effective lesson. Haus didn't trust me, and he revealed not only my limits but also his own when I failed to give him the proper guidance. It was a lesson I learned only by doing, and it's at the heart of the folly of all the poor decisions made by those who do not understand how to work with dogs.

Jakubin came into the bathroom and relieved me of Haus's leash. The dog couldn't get away from me fast enough. Jakubin was amused. "Not so easy, is it?" he asked.

19

If you know what to listen for, the sound is unmistakable. The attuned human ear can hear when a dog has found a sought-after odor, long before he gives his final alert. Depending on the training and the kind of detection work, a dog will either sit at the source of odor or lie down on the ground. A search-and-rescue dog will bark. A practiced handler will recognize his dog's personal tells. The dog may twitch his ears or his movements may slow down and become more deliberate, or he may even have an "I'm definitely on odor" expression, but it's really the sound that is the big giveaway. It's the deep, staccato inhale and then the rush of a heavy exhale. It is the sound of satisfaction. It is the sound of discovery.

The canine nose is a masterful creation. All earthly noses are not created equal, anatomically speaking. The average dog has roughly 220 million scent receptors in his nasal cavity. The average human has around 5 million. The canine sense of smell is 1,000 times more sensitive than a human's.

Even the way a canine nose functions is more developed than ours. A dog's nose has four passages, two inner ones and two outer ones. The inner canals pull in a scent and then the outer ones exhale it. The exhaling air doesn't disturb the ground or source of the next odor. This nose structure allows a dog to have an ongoing intake of fresh scent. Humans, in contrast, have just the two nasal passages. What goes up comes back out again the same way.

Dogs are trained to use their noses to make a memory of a smell. This is how a dog learns to seek out bombs, weapons caches, narcotics, missing persons, and, sadly, human remains. The process involves training a dog to associate odors with a reward. Dogs become visibly excited when they've discovered an odor they have been trained to detect. Less disciplined dogs will cast their heads back, looking, waiting, and watching for the treat-filled, rubber Kong (or tennis ball, or other treat) they know is coming, too eager to contain themselves.

In this age of modern warfare and police work, dogs are also trained to detect homemade explosives. These bombs are potluck-style concoctions, and while the recipes vary greatly, the ingredients are basically the same. So each dog is trained on a handful of key bomb-making ingredients. The catalog of explosive scents includes TNT, smokeless powder, potassium chlorate, C-4 plastic explosive, detonating cord, and ammonium nitrate.

In order for military-trained detection dogs to become certified, military regulations require that they meet a very high accuracy rate. Explosive-detection dogs must have a 95 percent accuracy rate. Drug dogs must be accurate at least 90 percent of the time.

The key to this kind of training is repetition and reinforcement. Maintaining proficiency at such a high rate requires a minimum of four hours of explosive-detection training a week. Whether this rate of accuracy also is reached in combat has not been proven and may be impossible to quantify. This is at least in part due to the fact that there really is no way to assess how many bombs or bomb materials go undetected, unless they go off after a dog team has cleared an area. In a controlled environment, when planted materials of any kind are used in training, their hiding spots are marked and known, and therefore those finds *can* be quantified.

20

Imagine a leaf floating down a creek. Shiny and wet, it winks out from the moving water. At first the leaf spins in lazy, looping circles, around and around like a carnival ride. Then it meets with a new current, picks up speed, and travels much farther and faster than you thought possible. Powerful, unpredictable, this is the finicky prerogative of the wind.

A rocky, dry path in the desert doesn't much resemble a stream, but when the wind passes through the dust, moving around clusters of shrubs and bushes, you can imagine how the analogy of a leaf on moving water captures the movement of scent on air. This is the sensory path a dog must follow, with all the obstacles in between. The shrubs would be like rocks in the water, parting the current and creating little eddies or pockets of scent. When a dog following scent across the desert floor comes upon a bush, he might pause and sniff around a little more, exploring the eddy created by wind, searching for a stronger pool of the odor he is tracking.

In order to harness the power of a dog's natural scent ability, a handler has to understand how a dog reads a scent trail, because it's the handler's job to assist the dog by tracking the wind. Because air is always flowing in the open space of the desert, all a handler needs to do is toe the earth and watch the dust lift to see which way the wind is going. Some handlers carry a spray bottle so they can punch a mist of water into the air and use that to detect the wind's intensity and direction. It's important that a handler has a good grasp on the direction of the wind because he needs to be able to "see" not what but *where* his dog is smelling.

The majority of dog teams dispatched to combat theaters are trained to find mortar shells, C-4, detonation cords, and pressure plates under the desert sand and brush, the components insurgents employ in their destructive IEDs. Pressure plates have become increasingly common. Insurgents bury these plastic disks, the size of dessert dishes, just under the surface of roads. When the weight of armored vehicles rolls over one, the little plate clicks upward and a bomb or mine hidden within it explodes.

To find such deadly weapons, handlers and explosive-detecting dogs need to be prepared, focused. In addition to keeping watch on the wind and on his dog, a handler must also keep his eye on the ground and the path ahead. By watching for disturbances that include wires, rock piles, and things that do not belong, as well as any other sign of human interference, the handler adds the keenness of the human eye to the power of the dog's extraordinary nose.

21

While no technology yet can match a dog's ability to detect odor—especially when it's a dog in a combat arena doing bomb detection work—that doesn't mean that scientists and technology developers and vendors have not been trying to outdesign Mother Nature's canine nose. Groups of private contractors and researchers at universities have attempted—and are likely still attempting—to do this, at the request of the military.

In the mid-1990s, the Defense Advanced Research Projects Agency initiated its "Dog's Nose Program" to make a bionic version of a dog's nose. It backed the venture with $25 million. As *Discover Magazine* reported in its September 2001 issue, two companies were in the running to develop this technology. Each took a slightly different approach. The first company, run by a neuroscientist at Tufts University, sought to create a "true electronic nose, capable of distinguishing a large variety of smells." The other company, called Flir Systems, partnered with Nomadic, Inc. They focused on TNT and DNT, two specific materials used to make explosives, and created Fido, the first "artificial nose capable of sniffing out a land mine in the real world."

Results, however, were mixed. As one of the Tufts researchers said in 2001, what they produced was "probably about a factor of 10 times less sensitive than the best dogs, but about par with the worst dogs." This was hardly a glowing appraisal, and hardly a ringing endorsement for the mechanical answer to the dog.

New versions of Fido persist. Fido X3 is advertised on the Flir website as the "next generation of threat detection." Its promoters are no longer trying to sell these devices as *replacements* for dogs but, instead, as an *additional* resource for base detection work. Amy Rose, the product sales director at Flir, told the *New York Times,* "We see our technology as complementary to the dog. Dogs are awesome. They have by far the most developed ability to detect concealed threats." But, Rose continued, "dogs get distracted, cannot work around the clock and require expensive training and handling."

Army dog handler Staff Sergeant Taylor Rogal has had experience with bomb dogs, but he's also worked with electronic bomb-detecting handheld devices. Most soldiers, if they don't have dogs with them when they conduct searches, use sensors like Fido. But Rogal said they have a reputation for breaking easily or being too sensitive to humidity and sand, which can render them ineffective. Rogal would rather put his trust in a dog—even a dog who's tired, thirsty, or hungry and has had a bad day.

When Rogal was deployed to Qatar in 2009, he and his detection dog, a German shepherd named Teri, worked security at the gate to their base. One time while they were on duty, a civilian drove onto the base, and Teri gave him a standard search before they let him through. But then, to Rogal's surprise, Teri paused and sat. He was on odor. Teri could be a stubborn dog, but Rogal knew that this was the dog's serious, no-kidding response: There was something in that car. So Rogal called it in.

When EOD came to investigate, Rogal's squadron commander, Lieutenant Colonel Gregory Reese, came to watch. It was a nerve-wracking few minutes for the handler, who was worried he had shut down gate access for nothing. But he trusted his dog. And while there wasn't a bomb, Teri's response was still a good one. EOD confirmed there was explosive residue in the car. The driver, a contractor who worked with explosive materials, hadn't cleaned the car properly. The find was a testament to the dog's powerful nose. The lieutenant colonel was impressed.

Rogal felt lucky to have a commander who supported the dog teams, one who would weigh this support against his reputation one day when a vendor came out to the base touting a Fido sensor. The man sold his product hard to the men in the group gathered around him, promising that the little handheld sensors would soon be all the detection help they needed. Rogal was watching from off to the side with another handler. He saw Lieutenant Colonel Reese join the group around the vendor.

To demonstrate the sensor's effectiveness, the salesman took out a sample of C-4 and pressed it against his thumb. He walked over to the bathroom trailer wall and pressed the same thumb against the side of the building. After that, he pulled out Fido and ran it over the trailer wall. A *ding* sounded. The machine had detected the minuscule amount of explosives.

Reese chuckled and told the vendor their dogs could do that, and just as fast. The vendor scoffed. Reese called over to the handler next to Rogal. "Go grab Hhart," he told him. The handler came back with Hhart, his search dog, and walked him over to the trailer, following a standard search pattern. As soon as they hit the spot with the thumbprint, the dog sat.

The vendor was visibly taken aback that the dog had performed so well and so quickly. It was clearly not what he had expected. Reese, on the other hand, gave him a satisfied smirk.

Being a handler, Rogal knows that he comes to this debate with a bias. But when he thinks back to standing guard on that gate, watching Teri give a fast and clear alert on just residual odor, there's no question in his mind which he would choose if given the chance. All Teri did that day was stick his nose in the car, and that, Rogal said, took just two seconds. And for Rogal, those extra seconds could mean the difference between life and death.

22

John Lutenberg, a former military dog handler, has been training bloodhounds and other dogs to track and trail for decades. Among the wide variety of jobs he's had, he has used dogs in Kenya to help officials hunt down poachers, and he has chased down escaped convicts for the Federal Bureau of Investigation.

At Jakubin's invitation, Lutenberg came to Fort Carson Army Base to show me his bloodhounds. With his fellow handler Terry Brown, Lutenberg brought Vicky out from the back of their truck. The dog's velvety coat drooped from her body. Her ribs showed and her jowls swung. A signature feature of the bloodhound breed, her loose skin flapped along her body with every long-legged move she made.

The bloodhound is, without question, the dog breed with the greatest scent ability. The bloodhound has on average 300 million scent receptors.

The way a trail dog like Vicky follows scent on air is different from how an explosive-detection dog might uncover an IED along a road or how a combat tracker dog would hunt down an insurgent, by mapping out a path and tracking odor on the ground. Many of the same components are at play—following the wind, standing on odor—but it is a different skill, and the dogs are trained in distinct ways.

Lutenberg crouched down and pulled one long finger through the rosy dirt, drawing what looked like a triangle without a bottom, the point facing up. This is the scent cone, he said. Then he dragged his finger across the dirt, starting at the base of the cone. He moved from left to right, going higher and higher until his finger ran out of space inside the cone and hit the top of the triangle at its smallest point. He was demonstrating how a dog moves to catch a scent on the air. The dog moves back and forth, closing in on her target until she lands right on top of it, right at the tip of the cone.

That is how Vicky found Jakubin, who, acting as the runaway decoy, had gone ahead of us, marking his trail with little orange ribbons. He finally positioned himself somewhere among the brush and trees where our eyes wouldn't find him before Vicky's nose did.

Trailing scent on air is fast-paced work that requires endurance. As soon as Vicky was on scent, she was on the move and she was moving *fast*. Because she was following scent with her nose in the air and didn't need to keep her nose to the ground, she ran freely. Brown, Vicky's handler, was keeping pace with her, holding onto her long lead and charging ahead of us on the uneven, rocky terrain. Lutenberg managed an equally brisk pace behind them.

When they finally reached the slight incline below Jakubin's hiding spot, Vicky made a wide swing turn and dodged right past Jakubin, as if she didn't see him. But a split second later, she made another sharp turn and bounded right on top of him, as he was curled up in a fetal position on the ground.

Lutenberg mapped out a replay. The wind was pushing to the right. This tossed Jakubin's scent out and away from him. "She got right here," he said, pointing to the spot in the air where Vicky made her pivot. "And she smelled him: 'He's right here, he's right here.'" Lutenberg's voice rose in soft excitement as he imitated Vicky, or at least how he imagined she would sound if she were able to talk.

Vicky, he explained, didn't *see* Jakubin because, above all else, dogs use their noses, not their eyes, for detection.

After she found him, Vicky wrestled around with Jakubin. Her eyes were hard to read buried under the soft wrinkles, but by the way her tail beat the air, it was clear she was pleased with herself.

23

While dogs are "nose strong," it would be a mischaracterization to say they have bad vision. One of the most popular misperceptions is that dogs are color blind. They're not. They just don't see as much color as we do. Also, when we measure their eyesight the way we measure human eyesight, with 20/20 vision as the standard, we come to the somewhat egocentric conclusion that dogs' eyes are inferior. But there are different ways to assess how dogs take in information with their eyes.

A dog's visual acuity (how well he is able to see defined details at a distance) is not as strong as a human's and not nearly as a strong as a cat's. (Eagles actually win the prize on this in the animal kingdom, seeing four to five times better than humans.)

But there's more to vision and interpreting information with one's eyes than acuity. And though a dog's eyes may not be as sharp as our own, their overall ability to take in information with their eyes is perhaps much better than ours.

For one thing, most dogs (depending on the breed) have a much wider field of vision, at 250 to 270 degrees, than do humans, at about 180 degrees. For another, dogs see much better in low light and darkness than we do. A part of dogs' eyes called the *tapetum lucidum* acts like a mirror. It reflects light, which helps dogs see well in the dark. Dogs' eyes also have more light-sensitive cells, called rods, than do human eyes.

In 2002, the Department of Zoology at Tel Aviv University conducted a study to see whether a dog relies more on his nose or his eyes when detecting explosives. They took trained dogs and ran them through detection drills in different settings under varying amounts of light. The gist of their conclusion was that "sniff" always prevailed over "see."

When they are on the hunt, a dog's eyes are apparently more sensitive to moving objects than to stationary ones. The study also found that because of this, the nose is more reliable in seeking "prey" or, as the case may be, explosives.

So when we consider dogs' sensory prowess, we have to take into account not only *how* dogs see but why. Perhaps they don't use their eyes as much because they don't need to. In this way, handler and dog dovetail nicely together—one sees while the other smells.

24

You know for sure that you've arrived at the ISAK course when you see a bright-yellow caution sign that bears the black outline of a dog. It is posted at the entrance to a dusty gravel parking lot.

As I walked across that parking lot after I arrived at 4:50 a.m., it was dark and cold and the only light came through the open door of an aluminum-roofed hangar. Marine Sergeant Charlie Hardesty, ISAK's lead instructor, emerged on his way to the training field to join the physical training course. The dog and handler teams were already there, hopping over and under a series of obstacles in full gear.

A chorus of howls sounded nearby. I glanced at Hardesty. He smiled a wide, mischievous smile. "Yep," he said, reading my mind. "Those would be the coyotes." I learned that, in addition to coyotes, an assortment of deadly snakes also slithered through the vicinity.

Gunnery Sergeant Kristopher Reed Knight, the course manager, arrived and walked over to where we were standing. He and Hardesty talked through the plans for the day. Hardesty was on his way to plant explosives for the first tactical training exercise. The sun was starting to rise and, with it, the temperature. There was a full day ahead for these handlers and their dogs, a day of looking for bombs.

For an instructor who was teaching handlers to search for explosives outside the wire, Hardesty was dependably cheerful.

He possessed a certain kind of purity of purpose and seeming wholesomeness. Each afternoon, after the day of tactical training was over, Hardesty would stay to work the dogs and with handlers who needed, and were willing to accept, extra help. Like most Marines, he didn't tolerate laziness, and though his patience might have frayed from time to time, neither the long days nor any amount of poor showing by the dogs or their handlers dampened his positive attitude while I was there. Except once.

Army Sergeant Dontarie R. Russ and his dog, Uudensi, a tawny German shepherd, were running a detection drill with instructor Army Staff Sergeant Lee McCoy. Up to this point, Russ had been a standout in the class.

Russ worked through the exercises tighter than many of the other handlers. He downed to one knee before rounding corners and managed his weapon with experience. One afternoon when Russ was performing well, Uudensi started to alert on human odor, which in the job of finding explosives counts as a false response. Russ began to founder. Rather than call the dog off the distracting scent and get him to move forward with the search, Russ jerked the leash and gave a flat verbal correction. Uudensi had lost his focus, and he ignored his handler. The dog continued his frantic scratching at the ground.

Hardesty stepped in. "Be firm, Dad," he said. Russ attempted to call the dog off again, but the tone of his voice was unchanged. If anything, he sounded even less concerned. In a flash, Hardesty advanced fast in Russ's direction, his own voice suddenly hard and loud. His even temper changed to anger. "Call him back like your life depends on it!" he yelled.

Russ was completely thrown. When he short-armed the Kong throw for his dog a minute later, he got angry at having to retrieve it himself. Seeing Russ struggle, Hardesty's storm passed as quickly as it had come on. Lowering his voice, he

Sergeant Russ and MWD Uudensi, with spotter Staff Sergeant Joseph Tajeda training at YPG.

Credit: Rebecca Frankel

coached the handler through. The command for the dog to "come" needs to be absolute, Hardesty told him. The dog's urge to respond to his handler has to be stronger than the dog's desire to alert on odor and stronger even than his desire to get the reward he attaches to alerting on odor. In the heat of a search, when a handler needs to call the dog away from danger, that dog must respond without delay.

I couldn't tell exactly what had triggered Hardesty's angry outburst. Maybe he just didn't want to put up with a poor attitude. But Hardesty also knew what was waiting for Russ and Uudensi after they left Yuma. He knew better than most what could happen when a handler doesn't keep his eyes open and pay attention.

25

In retrospect, that painted red rock outside the compound entrance had been a dead giveaway. But at the time, Hardesty and the British paratroopers he was with hadn't noticed it. They had missed the Taliban's tip-off to the danger inside, because they were too busy getting shot at and running to take cover.

It was January 2010, and the men of this British Air Regiment had begun their mission at dawn. The frigid temperature had propelled them to move fast across the river and make their way through the desolate fields up to the main market some three miles from their patrol base.

Hardesty and his combat tracker dog Robbie were with them. The dog team had joined this regiment at the start of their deployment, and Hardesty felt at home with them. These men had seen their fair share of firefights and had a gritty approach that Hardesty found appealing. And they had requested a combat tracker dog team, whose job required nerve, a lack of hesitancy, and a willingness to engage in swift-footed man-hunts. To Hardesty this meant they were willing to take risks.

The first part of their current mission was to reach out to the Afghans who lived in the area, to find new friends and identify potential enemies. For this they had invited the village elders in the area to a *shura,* a meeting over tea and bread, to discuss news of the Taliban.

The area they were in was wide open and rural, populated by clusters of different compounds. Each set of compounds was roughly 200 to 300 yards apart. Intel had gotten back to their unit that there might be Taliban living in one of these compounds. So, while the *shura* continued, Hardesty and Robbie pushed out with a smaller team under the command of British officer Pete McCombe to patrol the other compounds and complete the second part of their mission.

Earlier in the day, they'd seen some children playing outside a compound. Because the inside looked strangely quiet, they marked that as their target and made their way over. But as soon as they started to cross the field in that direction, they started taking gunfire. The enemy was stationed somewhere across the field in a neighboring compound. They had seen the soldiers coming and had no intention of letting them get any closer.

Hardesty and the others started to run. Robbie galloped alongside them, keeping tight to his handler. They didn't stop until they raced through the open door of that compound, where they took cover behind its walls, out of the range of bullets.

Inside, the first priority was to figure out exactly where the enemy was. McCombe yelled to one of the men to climb onto the roof of a hut. But the guy had trouble hoisting himself up. So they tossed him a ladder, a 30-pound collapsible one they always had with them. But the ladder fell and hit the ground. It landed right on top of an IED. The explosion launched the ladder some 40 yards back into the air, a tail stream of shrapnel sailing out behind it.

The blast knocked Hardesty to the ground. Rock and debris slapped against his face. And then the lights went out. When he opened his eyes, it took a few minutes for things to come back into focus. Whether he was out for seconds or minutes, he couldn't tell, but as soon as he came to, he knew something was very wrong with his ear. There was no sound coming in on one side. It was completely muffled. All he could think was, *It's gone. It's gone.* He brought his hand up to the side of his face and found his ear intact but touched it over and over anyway, overwhelmed with the sensation that it had somehow detached from his body.

He could tell his dog was still by his side without even having to look. He knew Robbie was staying close to him, he could feel him. The dog had remained relatively calm during the blast but looked up at Hardesty, eyes round and fearful.

And that's when he saw McCombe, lying on the ground completely still. The shrapnel had hit him square in the face, made a bloody mess of his eye, and knocked him unconscious. Hardesty moved toward him. As he got closer, he saw McCombe's body spring back to work before his mind was fully conscious. McCombe drew deep, gut-dragging gasps of air back into his lungs.

The medic was instantly at McCombe's side. He wrapped the wounds on his face and set up an intravenous line (IV) to give him morphine. When McCombe finally came to fully, finding his eyes covered sent him into a panic. He started fighting the hands that were trying to help him.

"I can't see! I can't see!" he shouted, and tried to tear the bandages from his face. McCombe had been a boxer in England, and he was solidly built and strong. It took four men to hold him down, to keep him from fighting the medic off.

Shrapnel had hit Hardesty as well. A few small pieces had entered the back of his head. Another few went under his plate carrier. But with all the chaos and adrenaline, he barely noticed. He took a quick few moments and gave Robbie a more thorough check to make sure he wasn't injured. There wasn't any bleeding, nor were there any apparent breaks. The dog had been low enough to the ground that nothing hit him, but while Robbie continued to brave the sounds of the nearby bullets, Hardesty could see that the loud noises unnerved him.

They had called a medevac for McCombe and had started to make a plan for their exit when someone shouted, "Freeze! Freeze! Freeze!"

The blast had shaken the compound and the ground beneath it, shifting the sand. A circular pattern of what looked like another buried explosive revealed itself just behind Hardesty, less than five feet from where he had fallen after the initial explosion. When they ran a metal detector over it, the machine let off a shrill *beep*. It was another IED.

Outside, the firefight still raged, but it was too dangerous for the unit to remain in the compound, where there might be more IEDs. They marked the bomb's position so they could safely avoid it during the evacuation. Some of the guys in their unit went into the field and settled into a ditch to lay down some supporting fire. They yelled back and forth to each other across the field while Hardesty took the metal detector and swept the rest of the compound so the quick reaction force could come in to get McCombe.

It took them nearly a half hour to safely evacuate, after which they had to walk about three miles back to their operating base.

McCombe lost his left eye, and another guy, who was standing just to Hardesty's left when the IED exploded, lost an arm. It would be two weeks before Hardesty got his hearing back.

They found out later that the explosives had been sitting idle for several weeks. As the ground compacted over time and rain fell in the compound, the earth around the IED had changed its shape. As a result, only seven of the 20 pounds of buried bomb had blown up, and the blast had exploded straight up, rather than in an IED's typical outward-shooting trajectory.

You would think having an IED explode in front of him like that, ripping away at his friends, would make a handler hesitant, afraid even, to go back out on patrol. But for Hardesty, it had the opposite effect. "If it's my time to go, it's my time to go. We don't have control over squat. You think you do, but we don't," he told me. "Tomorrow you could get in a car accident—you're dead. It's that simple, it's that silly, it's that sad and stupid, but that's how fragile life is."

26

Only one combat tracker team came through Yuma during the March ISAK class I visited. Hardesty set up special drills for them, since their job in-country would be much different from that of a bomb detection team.

Hardesty stood at the entrance to the "mosque" in the K-9 village. It was just one of the 90-some structures that made up one of two massive training sites at YPG.

This village was built and modeled after a satellite image taken of an actual Iraqi village. It was staged with considerable detail for authenticity. The huts were built from mud and clay, just as they would be in the combat theater. Inside the village, there were a wide market lane, a number of alleys and courtyards, and a cluster of huts that formed their own kind of maze. Many of the buildings had two levels with access to their rooftops. In its entirety, this training area stretched over nearly 80 acres.

On this particular day, Hardesty was going to set a track and then give the handler a mission, a story with all the information needed to pick up that track. The story went like this: Rumors were spreading that locals were cooperating with US forces, alerting them to areas where explosives had been planted. Tension between village leaders and the Taliban was growing. Intel led Marines to find a bomb planted inside the village mosque, thankfully before it detonated. However, the insurgent who had planted it there had escaped undetected. US forces believed that this man had likely taken refuge in a nearby cluster of huts, but the streets were crowded with people, loud with the bustle of the day. The tracker's job was to find him.

I chewed on this information and looked out over the huts a short distance away. It was time to think like the enemy. Which route would he take? Where would he hide? I could feel Hardesty watching me expectantly. It was me. *I* was going to be the insurgent.

In about an hour's time, Marine Lance Corporal John W. Peeler and his combat tracker dog Lex would be hunting, or rather tracking, me, the insurgent, down. To lay a track, to leave a scent on the ground, is a pretty simple task. But there's more to it than just walking from one place to the next. Hardesty wanted to make sure Peeler and Lex conducted the most realistic search possible. So, taking on the mind-set of a Taliban insurgent was key. How would he have assessed the scene in front of us? How would he have navigated the rolling mounds of rocky desert and the cluster of small one-room dwellings?

Tracking a person is essentially a fast-moving manhunt in which dog, handler, and the team working with them must stay close together. It's a footprint-to-footprint search in which a team has to abandon caution to push fast and far outside the boundaries of relative safety. This means closing the gap between human bodies and unexpected danger, which can include booby traps, trip wires, and/or the enemy lying in wait.

As we walked, I twisted around to see what kind of imprint I was leaving behind me. I could barely make out the pattern of the underside of my shoes. Their markings were faint against the pebbly ground, and they crossed paths with whoever else had been out there. But my track, whether visible or not, was quite strong. Aside from footprints and whatever odor we emanate in our wake, our trail is mostly made up of skin cells. We unknowingly cast off epidermal flakes everywhere we go. It's like Hansel and Gretel, only instead of bread crumbs, it's microscopic flesh droppings.

After the track was set, Peeler and Lex walked over the small wooden bridge near the mosque. Peeler had been a handler for only about a year and had been partnered up with Lex for about half that time. But he was completely self-assured when it came to his dog. One of the course instructors had complained that Peeler was *too* cocky. But to me, his excess of confidence was quieter. He had a settling of self that, at 24 years old, made him seem older.

Hardesty fed Peeler the story about the runaway insurgent and then outlined the objective: Find the bomber. Peeler knelt down to Lex and pulled the harness onto his back, a preparation that signaled to the dog that it was time to go to work, time to hunt. The change in Lex was instantaneous. He looked energized, ready to go. Next, Peeler hooked a long leash around the back of his own neck, behind his back, and under his arms so it rounded to the front. He wore gloves and let the leash slip through his hands as fast as Lex pulled it. It laced through his loosely closed hand like a zip line, until he decided Lex had gone far enough. Then he finally grasped and held the leash, applying a certain amount of resistance.

It's a technique Hardesty calls opposition reflex, and it's unique to tracking and trail work. Putting tension on the leash and adding that extra pulling sensation only fuels a dog's drive to push harder. It's all about the reward, about the toy the dog knows is waiting for him at the end of the track. According to Hardesty, the dog knows from doing this time and time again that if he pulls hard enough and smells that odor on the ground long enough, he's going to get his reward.

Unlike in IED detection work, where military handlers have had great success working their dogs off the leash, in combat tracking, it's essential that the handler and the dog maintain a taut-leash tension between them. In tracking, Hardesty explained, the amount of odor you're following is very small and supersensitive. Giving a dog a correction or command at the wrong time could too easily throw him off the track.

Peeler began by scanning the ground to find his starting point. It was the spot where I had dug hard with my heel into the ground. He directed Lex's nose to that spot, and with a perk of Lex's ears, the chase was on. Lex's nose worked hard. The sounds of his panting, inhaling and exhaling, were audible. He was a dog intent, moving with controlled frenzy.

For a tracker dog, Lex had a deliberate style and he worked at a moderate pace. While Lex ambled a little ways away from the path we tracked, Peeler was looking at the ground. He held his position and only allowed Lex to pull the slack of the leash.

Lance Corporal John Peeler and his combat tracker dog Lex at YPG in March 2012.

Credit: Rebecca Frankel

A tracker dog handler has to focus not only on his dog, but he must scan for signs of disturbance as well as other clues along the way.

Hardesty and I followed from a distance. I didn't want to get too close. I wanted Lex to focus on the scent trail I had left on the ground. After some fast moving, we made an abrupt stop. Lex lifted his head and Hardesty gave me a nudge. "Dog cast his head up," Hardesty whispered. He explained that this is a sign to the handler that his dog has lost the scent. Peeler peered at the ground hard, his expression impossible to read. The ground was a maze of messy earth. Each patch looked nearly identical. If he saw anything noteworthy among the scuffs and pebbles, he didn't reveal it.

As the moments passed, Peeler remained calm and un-hurried. He pulled Lex back a few feet and to the left, to the last spot where the dog had been really pulling him on scent. They held there, steady, almost still for a few breaths, the leash between them taut. Within a few seconds, Lex's nose hit the ground and they were back on the move, this time even faster than before.

Lex didn't stop moving until we reached the spot where I had kicked out another small divot of earth to mark the end of the track. Hardesty had planted a tennis ball, Lex's reward, on the same spot. Peeler whooped to praise his partner on a job well done. Lex took his prize and hunkered down with it inside one of the small huts out of the sun.

27

The following week, I would leave another track across the gravelly Yuma desert, but this time there weren't any dogs following me. Instead, I was following the dogs through an eight-mile ruck march. Staff Sergeant Christopher Keilman, one of the course instructors, had helped me kit up. He tightened the Velcro shoulder straps of the Kevlar vest and cinched the ones that wrapped around my rib cage, working to get the snuggest fit possible. He apologized when it still brushed so low it tapped against my hipbone. The plate carrier, which belonged to a male instructor, weighed somewhere between 15 and 20 pounds. I could still fit my backpack over the vest. It contained, among other things, my notebooks, warmer layers (which it turned out I would have no need for), and four bottles of cold water. This all weighed around 12 pounds.

Keilman then handed me the heavy, red, rubber training rifle that weighed roughly seven pounds. He quickly corrected my instinct to keep my fingers hovering over the trigger. Apparently, that was bad. When I relaxed my arms and let the rifle go slack, it pointed at my toes. "You can't let it hang down," he warned. This was also bad, as it increased the likelihood that, were this a real gun with real bullets, I might quite literally shoot myself in the foot. "You have to keep your weapon at the ready," he said, pulling the gun's barrel upward. I adjusted my grip to keep it straight, my forearms instantly twitching.

After doubling up some of the magazine clips on my vest, Keilman took a step back to look me over. Seeing no other room for improvement, he shrugged and went to join the other instructors who were already outside.

The dogs were fidgety while their handlers tugged on their leashes to keep the line formation. The teams stood in two rows flanking the left and right of the road. Each dog team had to keep a distance of about six feet or so from the team ahead of it. The dogs needed their space from one another, mostly to keep the more aggressive dogs from fighting. Some had muzzles on.

There had been a few dogs who were struggling earlier in the course, and I picked them out. Jeny, Jessy, and Turbo. I knew watchful eyes would be swept in their direction all night.

An expectant energy prickled in the air. Boots shuffled. The dogs were twisting, ready to move. Finally, Kitts shouted over the din of low chatter and the jostling gear, and the march began.

It was then that I began to feel the actual weight of what I was doing. It was as if the vest and backpack were straining to meet the ground, threatening to take me with them. All together, I was still carrying only about half the weight the handlers were. Their packs, which included extra water for their dogs and plate carriers, averaged around 70 pounds. The troop was moving at a rigorous clip, a speed that, even without the gear, would have registered for me as a steady jog.

I stopped to adjust the straps on my pack and looked up. I was alone, already trailing way behind. The only thing behind me was a big white pickup truck driven by the veterinary technician. In the truck, Captain John Brandon Bowe rode shotgun.

That I was ahead of the truck was nothing to be proud of. It was their job to keep up the rear in case any of the dogs or handlers were injured or too fatigued to finish the march. If anything, I was the reason they were going so slowly.

They pulled up alongside me. Bowe, a Marine and executive officer of the Military Police Instruction Company and the ISAK course's school director, leaned out the open window and called over to ask me how I was doing. "You know," he said, his eyebrows crooked with concern, "I won't think any less of you if you don't do it." We were barely 20 minutes into the ruck. There were miles of tougher ground still to cover, including the incline leading to the tower, the site that marks the midway point. At the top of the hill, the teams would break for a short rest and the handlers would water the dogs, take their temperatures, and collectively catch their breath.

I felt the sweat trickling down my back and chest. I looked at the empty, air-conditioned, inviting backseat. My fingers were cramping, but I tightened them around the gun in my hands and shook my head. Bowe gave me a dubious look but assented, and I pushed ahead of them on the road, willing my unwilling muscles to put some distance between us.

The evening began with the ruck that would lead the teams to the K-9 village, which is where the nighttime missions would begin. They were designed to be as similar as possible to the soon-to-be-very-real assignments the teams would be given downrange. It was the third and final week of the ISAK course, when training begins every day just before sundown. It would also be the last night of "hand-holding" before the students and dogs would run drills without the instructors walking alongside them.

28

About an hour into the march, modest relief came on a teasing breeze, one that promised a mild night. It was a good sign for everyone, including the dogs, as many of them, whose home stations were in cooler or more humid climates, were unaccustomed to steady exercise in such dry heat. But after Yuma, steady heat was what awaited these teams as they deployed to Afghanistan or Iraq. Up ahead, the sky turned a buttery orange. The silhouettes of handlers and dogs blackened against the horizon, like upright shadows.

Knight kept a brisk pace behind the last handler. He had brought along his dog, Max, a Belgian Malinois puppy he was training privately. Max was tireless, determined, and a favorite playmate of all the instructors. He would nose his way into the classroom during briefings to drop a slobbery tennis ball on an unsuspecting lap, ever poised for the chase. On this night, while the other dogs were in work mode, focused and marching in sync with their handlers, Max was off his leash and bounding ahead of Knight. He dipped on and off the road, his big ears flopping out of rhythm with his wild, young-dog energy.

"Look at him," Knight called over, unabashedly proud of his rambunctious charge. "He could do this whole march at that pace and *still* not be tired."

Knight did not have a reputation for being a warm, fuzzy type. He was known instead for the lengths he would take to enforce his high, uncompromising standards. I had heard a

Marine Gunnery Sergeant Kristopher Reed Knight wrestles with Max, in March 2012.

Credit: Rebecca Frankel

story about a handler from Buckley Air Force Base who had orders to fill an instructor position at YPG under Knight's command. But when Knight found out that she had no outside-the-wire experience, he called and told her not to bother coming. In his mind, without having done it herself, she couldn't offer anything worthwhile to handlers on their way to war, and therefore she was of no use to him. Supposedly, the movers had been there at her house, packing her stuff, while this conversation took place, but it hadn't mattered. He didn't want her, so she wasn't coming.

Though he didn't say so, I suspected Knight was walking the eight-mile ruck with Max to keep an eye on me. If there's one person I didn't want to see me struggle through this march, it was Knight. Right after I put on the gear, he had passed me in the hangar and watched me pop a stick of gum into my mouth. "Huh," he had smirked. "That gum's not gonna save you."

But now that we were moving, Knight was my only company. He shouted again for Max, who, like a tiny gazelle, popped back into sight from behind a sloping mound of sand. His pink tongue flapped out of his mouth to the side, and his eyes were alight with the excitement of adventure.

As the midway point of the ruck came into view, all I could see was a mountain, a big, insurmountable rise in the earth coated in slippery pebbles and loose sand. I watched a couple of handlers shoot up to the top, pushing themselves through the worst of the steep hill, their dogs panting but bullying their way up alongside them. No one fell. I did not want to be the first to do so. "You ready for this?" Knight asked me with his sly-dog grin. I just shook my head in his direction as we took the first few steps, and tried to laugh as if I were having the time of my life, but I was breathing so hard I sounded more like a horse choking.

"Here," Knight said, holding out Max's leash. The puppy was making wheezing sounds similar to my own, but he was actually yanking hard to race to the top. I could not keep pace with him. I shook my head again. I was starting to question

Knight's motives, wondering if the instructors had taken bets on when I would pass out and if we'd just hit his payout mark.

But Knight put the leash in my hand and pushed my shoulder. "Lean back," he told me in a low voice. And suddenly my addled brain caught on. Max, beautiful, inexhaustible Max, so desperate to get to the other dogs, was going to pull me with the force of a tractor-trailer all the way to the top. I used my weight to counterbalance his tugging, and all I had to do was hang on and lift my feet. We smoked past the other teams trudging their way up the hill, hurtling with the grace of a tiny tornado through the middle of the road.

At the top of the hill, handlers and dogs rested, each pair separated a modest distance from the others. The group was quiet for once. It felt symbolic to see each handler alone with his or her dog, just as they would be on an actual mission. A team of two.

Staff Sergeant Robert Wilson knelt in front of his dog Troll. He took the dog's temperature while Bowe looked on. Peeler was sitting on the ground, his pack slumped up behind him still strapped onto his shoulders, and he leaned back into it, his weapon flat across his bent knees. Lex was on the ground by his ankles, the sides of his body moving as he took in each deep, rapid breath. Lance Corporal Eddie Garcia was about two yards down the slope from Peeler, his dog Lubus curled on his side against him. Lance Corporal Joshua Ashley was one of the few still on his feet, standing to the left of the truck. He was holding his gun at the ready. His dog Sirius had taken position by his boots.

Hardesty and McCoy made the rounds and checked in on the dogs. They watched the handlers take their dogs' rectal temperatures, water them down, and give them turns at the orange coolers placed nearby for a nice, long drink. Most everyone kept on his gear.

And then the day was gone. The sunset's blushing oranges had burned down into the horizon and a dusky purple had risen to color the sky. My eyes adjusted to the dark as the chem sticks that the handlers had on their backs and helmets began their neon glow.

Then the break was over. The ruck was back on.

29

Packs lifted, the descent began. Knight's trick to get me to the top with Max wouldn't work on the way down. I tried to copy the side-to-side steps of the handlers down the slant of the hill and to grip the hill with the bottoms of my feet.

At the end of the ruck march, the dog teams got ready for the night's missions. These drills would extend well into the morning hours. I limped my way over to wait with the instructors.

Keilman asked me how I felt. My bones ached. My knees, which had been reduced to unsteady knots, wobbled. My shoulders screamed for mercy. It felt like the places where my joints ought to meet no longer wanted to hold together. But my face stretched into a smile so big it was beyond my control. Keilman smiled back and told me he was proud. He raised his hand to give me a high five.

Knight and Max were waiting for me to walk the final yards, about the length of a football field, back to the hangar. But in a moment of adrenaline-fueled mania, I offered to take Hardesty's pack to the office for him. As he hoisted his 70-pound rucksack over my much smaller backpack, I teetered. My hips nearly gave out. But I smiled the smile of delirious triumph and sucked whatever air I could harness into my lungs. I can do this too, I told myself.

By the time I made it over to Knight, I knew I had made a terrible mistake. After taking one look at me, he knew it too. He pulled the pack off my shoulders and carried it the rest of the way.

30

The evening following the ruck was the first night of the ISAK course's final exams, or FINEX. Staff Sergeant William Stone was delivering his spotter's brief to McCoy before patrolling the market lane in ISAK's K-9 village. The brief included two lines, always said together, that every handler must know forward and backward: "Where I go, my dog goes. Where my dog goes, I go."

A handler also has hardwired in him instructions on how to handle the dog as well as the dog's equipment, which is with them at all times. In addition, handlers carry a card that they give to the medic before a mission. It lists basic emergency care for anyone who might be able to administer lifesaving measures if the dogs are injured downrange. Things that even a medic might not know—like, for example, that dogs require more morphine than humans.

Earlier that evening I'd walked the market lane with McCoy, and he had showed me where he had set up the plants. "Tonight's the rude awakening," McCoy had said.

It was the last night for practice, the last night to make mistakes. The instructors had purposely set the teams up for failure. The teams were getting more difficult exercises to jar the handlers out of any bad habits and complacency.

At one of the huts, McCoy had set up a trip wire drawn loosely along the base of the wooden door frame. It was so menacingly obscure it all but disappeared in the darkness.

McCoy stepped back, looked at the wire, and crossed his arms. He knew this was still the crawl phase for the handlers, but all too soon, he said, they would be running.

McCoy recalled his deployment to Afghanistan. In Uruzgan Province, there is a 10-mile-long thoroughfare known rather notoriously as IED Alley. McCoy, with his Specialized Search Dog Spalding, a chocolate Lab, had regularly patrolled the area. One day, after they received reports that there were IEDs on the road ahead, McCoy and Spalding pushed out and started doing a search with the Afghan National Army guards. After a while, McCoy saw that the dog was tired and needed a rest. No sooner had he grabbed Spalding and turned away than a bomb blew up. The blast knocked McCoy clear off his feet and Spalding onto his side. They had been only 20 feet from the explosion.

For this night's missions, the handlers used NVGs clipped to their helmets. Hardesty showed them how to balance them and weigh them down with batteries to keep them from sliding out of place. The NVGs were small and black, essentially half a pair of binoculars. The flap around the eyehole was soft black rubber that closed out all the light. I put them on and, after a few blinks, a fuzzy picture came into view, in which everything was colored in varying shades of neon lemon and lime green.

It's one thing to see through NVGs. It's another to actually know how to use them. McCoy demonstrated how to adjust them and pick out the trip wire. At first it was barely visible.
It lay flat in the dark. If you didn't know the wire was already
there, it would have been nearly impossible to see. But with a
twist of one of the NVGs' filters and a push of the infrared but-
ton, the wire popped into view, glowing white hot, like a thin
thread of crackling electricity. Now there was no way anyone
could miss it. This ability to unveil otherwise invisible dangers
felt like a secret defense, like Superman's X-ray vision.

Even so, that wire in McCoy's lane nailed almost all the
teams that came through that night.

During the mission, loud music blasted from the intercom system throughout the village, and there was a bonfire
raging in an oil drum, with flames blazing more than 10 feet

Lance Corporal Phil Beauchamp and his MWD Endy at YPG in March 2012.
Credit: Rebecca Frankel

into the air. The blast simulator emitted the noise of erupt-
ing mortar shells, and it sounded constantly. The combined
chaos was designed specifically for this night of training. It
created an added layer of stress that Marine Lance Corporal
Phil Beauchamp admitted threw him off. He said he "died"
twice within five minutes.

That night Beauchamp and his dog lost their groove. He
was annoyed with the dog and with everything else. "As soon
as you lose your attitude, everything goes downhill. And the
dog loses his attitude, too, when you lose yours. And I believe
in that," he said, his brown eyes serious. "You know, everything
that you feel, the dog feels."

They had actually been doing pretty well until McCoy's
lane. After that trip wire, Beauchamp got frustrated and just
lost it.

But just as McCoy said, failing this time was the whole
idea.

31

Few of the handlers who came through Yuma arrived ready
to hit the ground running. Neither did the dogs. Some
handlers had deployed before, but others were new handlers,
some of them just a couple of months out of Dog Training
School. Some hadn't picked up a weapon, a real weapon, since
basic training. Others had never even held NVGs before, let
alone been trained on how to use them properly. They were
meant to learn it all at YPG in three weeks.

And they are meant to make mistakes.

There was a lot more than tactical training going on. The instructors also imparted life lessons in the most basic sense of the word. Humility in the face of failure. Lessons on patience and tolerance. How to accept that some things cannot be rushed. How to accept that it might be your time. How to not be so afraid of getting hurt or dying that you worry yourself into failure when failure is not an option. If you fail, they teach, you die. And if it's not your time then, well, you still could be risking the lives of the people following behind you, the people who trust that when you say it's safe, it is truly safe to walk the road.

McCoy, Keilman, and Hardesty took the time to coach each handler who ran into trouble, especially those who took out their frustrations on their dogs. With the dogs, handlers have to stay positive, gentle, and patient. They should not rush. They should not breach doorways. They should not let their dog breach doorways. Each time handlers crossed that threshold and tripped the wire, McCoy pressed them as to why they were moving so fast. Were you given a time limit? he asked. The answer was always no.

That was exactly what McCoy asked Stone, when he and his dog Atos went through the lane and set off the trip wire. Take your time, McCoy told him. But Stone seemed unconvinced. "Even if we're in a hard knock?" he wanted to know.

McCoy was adamant. Even in a hard knock, he told Stone. Even, he said, if there are all types of crazy things going on, you, the handler, have to be firm and careful. You have to do a thorough search before crossing any door seams.

"Yes, sir. I'm not gonna die anymore," Stone said, making a stab at self-deprecating humor. But as far as McCoy was concerned, there was no room for jokes. He told Stone a story about what had happened to six men from the 1st Battalion,

75th Ranger Regiment, when he was with them in Afghanistan. The regiment didn't want to use the dog guys. And one day, when they came under enemy attack, these six soldiers ran into a building. They made it over the first threshold, he said, but the second threshold had a trip wire. All six were buried alive. All six died.

Stone was ready to go again. He gave McCoy a loud, firm "Yes, sir!" before he and Atos moved forward to the next section of the lane. McCoy instructed him to clear the building while skipping the courtyard, then to come out, hook left, and clear the left side of the lane. As Stone searched, it was clear he had taken McCoy's words to heart. They were in this part of the lane for a long time. Yet when Stone breezed through a corner, McCoy stopped him. Clearing a corner should be simple and methodic—high, low, square, deep—he told Stone. That way you don't miss anything. If Stone had taken the time to do this, he would've had the find even faster than he eventually did. McCoy shook his head. A lot of people try shortcuts, he said, "and shortcuts get people killed."

32

Despite the many likely hazards waiting for them in a war zone, most of the handlers were excited to get downrange. For some it would be their first deployment, while for others it would be their second, third, or even sixth. The high number was surprising, especially given how young they were. If they weren't actively excited to go back, they didn't seem to mind it.

If they had been to Iraq, they were looking forward to a tour in Afghanistan. They wanted to go.

The reason why many handlers joined up in the first place varied. A lot of them cited 9/11 or talked about doing their patriotic duty to serve their country. Others had relatives, fathers or grandfathers, who had served, and they were just following in step with a family legacy. For still others, reaching the combat theater promised a sense of completion. It was where they could put into practice all their training, all their hard work with their dogs. Many of them didn't want assignments working base patrol, manning military base entry and exit points, or conducting traffic checks. As far as they were concerned, these jobs were rote, boring. As far as they were concerned, these jobs weren't the point.

For handlers, the draw of deployment holds more than just the satisfaction of seeing through a successful mission with their dog or saving lives. Combat zone life is a rush. After Ashley and Sirius arrived in Afghanistan, Ashley told his older brother that going out on a mission was the best adrenaline high he'd ever had.

The intoxicating thrills of war aside, going downrange is the most intensely intimate time there is for a K-9 team. Combat-experienced handlers like Knight say it's the best time for the dogs, because they're with their handler upward of 20 hours a day. And it's the best time for a handler to learn everything he can about the dog.

Even Jakubin, who never deployed to a combat zone or worked outside the wire in Iraq or Afghanistan, admitted that he has mixed feelings of gratitude and envy when he thinks about what it would have been like if he had deployed to war. When he talked about this hole in his otherwise vast dog-handling experience, his voice was regretful, even as he acknowledged that it may well have been a blessing.

Kitts described being downrange with Dyngo as unlike anything he'd experienced on assignments in the States. It's where the trust a handler has in his dog is truly tested. By the time a team finishes all their training and gets downrange, the handler has to have confidence that his dog can and will find explosives. He has to trust his dog with his life. Walking outside the wire without that mentality could easily thwart a handler's chance of surviving.

Kitts remembered the first time he went outside the wire, the very first step. His stomach was full of butterflies, but for him it was like stepping out onto a sports field. Once he and Dyngo started working, everything fell into place and the nerves died down.

But inevitably, doubt can creep in and take hold of a handler. Knight said he's had students who've come to him to express fear about deploying, fear about being blown up. But there is no room for doubt with this job, Knight said, and so what he told them is: "Don't cry to me about it."

Hardesty more readily admitted that theirs was a daunting job. And a little bit of fear, he said, is healthy. But he agreed that if a handler is just straight scared, it isn't the job for him. A handler leading a patrol has to be mindful of his job and all the responsibility that comes with it. A handler has to accept that when he and his dog clear a path, there are lives on the line. "It's not about you," Hardesty said. "It's the guys coming up behind you. You're leading the way. You're the one making it clear or safe for everybody else to travel. That's a huge responsibility. If you aren't humble and honest with yourself and what you're really capable of, then you need to get . . . out of the way and let somebody else do it."

33

Sometime in the wee hours of that March morning, after the ruck, after the missions and hours of chaos in the K-9 village were nearly finished, the EOD crew came around to collect and lock away the explosive materials. Somehow, I felt wide awake. Hardesty and Kitts stood around, waiting for EOD to wrap up. They played songs from their cell phones, their faces lit with incandescent blues and whites.

I felt suspended between worlds, between the green halo of NVGs that still clogged my vision when I blinked and the cars parked just a few hundred yards away that would deliver us home. The sensation faded further as embers in the oil barrel died out, but the reality of what this preparation was all for, that place they'd all be going, was unmistakable. Tonight that distance between here and there had been pulled in closer, tightened like a stitch along a loose-fitting seam. Yuma is the place between places, somewhere between here and war.

34

In the constellation Canis Major you will find Sirius, the Dog Star. It is the brightest of all the stars in the night sky. The ancient Egyptians tracked the Dog Star, using its position to determine the rising of the Nile so that each year they would know when it was time to seek shelter on higher ground. It was fitting, then, that for FINEX, I followed Ashley and his dog Sirius. It was the last night of nights at Yuma.

The air was warm, balmy even. When he was clear on his instructions, Ashley began to give his pre-mission brief to Kitts and McCoy. He told them his call sign was going to be "Shrek," and Beauchamp, who was acting as Ashley's spotter, chimed in with his chosen sign, "Gingerbread Man." (He briefly considered but ultimately decided against using "Donkey.") Sirius stood close to Ashley, looking up as if he were listening to it all and then out again into the distance as if he were assessing their target. I heard my name and realized I would also be assigned a call sign: "Princess Fiona."

All the work of the previous three weeks was about to be tested. Instructors would observe from a distance and communicate only through walkie-talkies. Kitts drove the truck and McCoy rode shotgun, filling out the FINEX evaluation sheets on a metal clipboard. Hardesty sat in the back. The air in the car was a jiggling mix of something like parental anticipation, confined frustration, and midsummer-night mischief. Sitting in the car for eight hours observing from a distance was proving tedious. The instructors were wound up. There was more than a passing grade on the line.

These were the last hours they would have with their students, the last time they could impart any lessons to them, the last hours they could convey helpful instructions. It was their last chance to say the thing that might stick, the thing that might keep the teams from getting blown up in theater. The next day, their students would go off to the real thing. And the next time someone planted bricks of C-4 behind a wooden board in a hut, it wouldn't be an exercise like this one. It would be real life. Real life or death.

Ashley, Sirius, Beauchamp, and I set off. We took the road that led away from the kennels. All the lights across the area had been cut. It was a mandatory blackout. The moon was out of sight, nowhere to be found. Ashley set a confident pace. He, Sirius, and Beauchamp moved quickly, talking their way through the path ahead, deciding which route to take from the road to the palm grove that we were meant to search. They were both using their NVGs. I held mine tightly in my hand, reluctant to use them. Instead I trained my eyes on the men's feet. I watched the heels of their boots so I could follow their exact steps rather than forge my own route.

Marine Lance Corporal Joshua Ashley and his partner, MWD Sirius, look for buried aids during a training exercise at YPG in March 2012.

Credit: Rebecca Frankel

I had decided to shadow Ashley and Sirius in part because I had kept close watch on their tactical training throughout the course, but also because I trusted, from what I had seen so far, that Ashley would do a good job. We wouldn't, for example, spend 20 minutes heading in the wrong direction, as one team did. I was also certain that my presence wouldn't ruffle him. Another reason I chose to follow them was that I knew, with Beauchamp as the spotter, this team would be fun.

The palm grove came into view, and Ashley took a knee, scoping out the target, instructing Sirius to down. The dog dropped beside him. His obedience to his handler was quick, and their communication was easy and smooth. Sirius kept his eyes trained on his handler as Ashley radioed to "base command" and waited for the area to be "cleared."

A few explosions sounded, followed by bursts of light. This was achieved with a remote-controlled blaster in the SUV. The booms were simulated but powerful. Ashley got the okay from Kitts to move forward.

We left the road and moved onto uneven ground. Beauchamp turned back to make sure I didn't pitch and fall. He cautioned me to watch my step. I squinted and squished my eyes, trying to pinch whatever light I could out of the night. I realized I wasn't going to make it far without the NVGs after all. The NVGs shifted my depth perception when I put them on, and I stumbled and dropped before my eyes adjusted. My uneven footsteps made sounds as the bottom of my shoes scraped against the sand and stone.

The palm grove was the only irrigated spot at YPG's K-9 course, and as we approached, it lifted in front of us like a mirage, lush even in the dark, the palm fronds bending with the wind. The huts inside were squat, square structures that, in the daytime, were orange and dusty, just like all the others in the nearby K-9 village. Here they felt almost tropical.

In the dark, I was disoriented. I could hear Beauchamp, Ashley, and Sirius moving around, but I worried that I wouldn't be able to find them. It seemed only too easy to get turned around in this filtered nighttime world, to lose one's sense of direction entirely, even in the small palm grove. There was the sound of trickling water and the ghoulish white of the night sky reflecting in enormous puddles that broke up the ground.

Ashley worked methodically, his voice low and melodic as he coaxed the dog through the search, while Beauchamp called out helpful directions, reminding him of doorways, letting him know which ways were clear. And then Ashley sent Sirius into the hut.

Earlier in the day, I had watched Hardesty and Kitts stack explosives, little blocks that resembled oversized sardine cans, in the hut. They completely filled the bottom of a window frame. Sirius moved under the "hot" window, and his response was swift. The dog lowered his haunches, his hindquarters sank in slow motion until his tail finally met the ground. He cast a look back at his handler. They had found it.

"This is Gingerbread Man," Beauchamp said into his radio. He alerted the instructors that they had a positive response, identified the location of the hut, and requested EOD backup.

Kitts's voice came back over the radio. The find was good, the first part of the mission complete. Ashley and Beauchamp relaxed and walked down a deep slope and back up the road toward the K-9 village.

The next leg of the mission included a search of a building with low beams and plywood walls where the bats flew so low that everyone had to duck their heads. Kitts and McCoy were waiting outside when we arrived. McCoy came around to Ashley. "You did good, man," he told him. "You did good."

Ashley and Sirius passed that night of FINEX with a mark of 100 percent. And that is what came to my mind months later when the unthinkable happened.

part three

what's love got to do with it?

35

Inside the world of handlers and their working dogs is a culture of dedication and sacrifice, even grief, all the things one might expect to find. But there was something else I encountered, something surprising.

Resistance to the idea of love.

Kevin Howard sat in a collapsible mesh chair along with a few handlers from Jakubin's kennels and two other former military dog handlers. The group was taking a lunch break from decoy work at Fort Carson. We picked at paper plates of pulled-pork sandwiches and coleslaw, using the open truck beds for seats and tabletops. The conversation meandered through many topics.

Then Howard said that he doesn't believe dogs show a true preference for their individual handlers. He doesn't believe his dogs love him. Nor does he believe that the emotion we call "love" has a place in working with dogs. Affection maybe. But not love. Instead, he feels a dog is driven by a will to survive and to make puppies.

To understand dogs, he explained, you first have to understand that dogs exist within the dynamics of a wolf pack. Wolf pack speak is commonplace within the MWD program. The handler, Howard said, should be seen as the alpha male, as a benevolent dictator, the person in charge who rules with cement-like consistency. The rules are hard and fast. If the dog stays within the preset boundaries, he will be rewarded and protected. If, however, the dog breaks these rules, there are consequences, just as there would be in a wolf pack.

In Howard's view, it would be considerably worse for a handler to forget his position in the pack and treat his dog like a pet than it would be for a handler to show little or no emotional attachment to his dog. Treating a dog with too much affection is detrimental for an MWD, Howard said, because it ultimately undermines the dog's sole purpose, which is to serve.

However, the long-popular wolf theory of dominance is now commonly considered to be an outdated model for analyzing canine behavior. It doesn't stand to reason, as author Alexandra Horowitz points out in her book *Inside of a Dog,* that just because dogs descended from wolves, all of their ancestors' attributes have transferred. More limiting, she argues, is the "faulty premise" of the "pack." The real model of wolves is not a pack but a family. "In the wild, wolf packs consist almost entirely of related or mated animals. They are *families,* not groups of peers vying for the top spot." Breaking down wolf (and subsequently dog) behavior into a "linear hierarchy with a ruling alpha pair and various 'beta' and even 'gamma' or 'omega' wolves below them" is just too simplistic.

But there's clearly an appeal to the idea that dogs organize themselves like a wolf pack, where some lead and others follow. As Horowitz observes, it allows us to suppose that we are "dominant and the dog submissive." And, perhaps because they're influenced by the tiered structure of the military, military handlers still frequently teach, refer to, or live by the dominance hierarchy of the wolf pack when training and working their dogs. This leaves little room for the idea that dogs have a sophisticated set of emotions or that they possess the ability to love freely or choose whom it is that they love.

Jakubin, who was standing nearby, nodded along in agreement as Howard made his case. I found this startling, given all he has said about how real grief and real mourning accompanies the loss of each dog. But he didn't contradict Howard, and neither did any of the other handlers. The consensus of this group was that in the relationship between working dog and handler, there is more function than feeling. They seemed to readily agree that whatever is exchanged between man and dog, that thing is not love.

36

On Staff Sergeant Pascual Gutierrez's first day of K-9 school, one of the instructors told the class, "Your dog is a weapon. Your dog is not a pet. Do not get close to your dog. Do not grow attached to your dog." That first-day lesson was one he accepted. He considers it an important bottom-line truth, vital to the integrity of being a good handler. Inside this instruction is a cautionary tale: A handler who is too emotionally attached to his dog is more likely to make an irreparably poor combat zone decision if he does so with his heart and not his head.

When I met him, Gutierrez was a handler under Jakubin's command at the USAF Academy kennels. And, like all handlers, Gutierrez readily acknowledged that the business of MWD teams is to save human lives, sometimes at the expense of canine lives. Gutierrez accepted that in a scenario where his life, or the lives of the men and women walking behind him, was to be weighed against the life of his dog, human life would always take priority. And it was this long-prepared mentality

Staff Sergeant Pascual Gutierrez and Mack compete during the K-9 trials at Lackland in May 2012.

Credit: Rebecca Frankel

that he was going to bring with him to his sixth deployment in Afghanistan, his second as a canine handler. This time around he was going downrange with a relatively green dog, Bert, a Belgian Malinois with a high work drive. Bert was an aggressive, unpredictable type who liked to bite.

After spending 43 days at the Air Force's relatively new pre-deployment course, Gutierrez and Bert had only just begun to mesh. Gutierrez was pleased. He felt that Bert had finally reached the point where the dog accepted that he was his "dad."

This familial classification is standard speak inside the MWD training program. Handlers refer to themselves as "moms" and "dads," especially when identifying the dog's point of view. During drills and exercises, handlers are never "master" or "keeper," "handler" or "trainer." They are always referred to in this parental terminology. It's natural. Handlers are responsible for their dogs in the most basic ways and, by virtue of their occupation, are primarily caretakers. They feed their dogs, bathe them, give them exercise, and keep them in good health. So, referring to them in terms of guardianship feels appropriate.

But this terminology is one of many conflicting details in defining what a dog *is* to his handler: weapon, comrade, soldier, tool, or child. And it doesn't help answer the question of why love would have to be omitted from the handler-dog relationship.

I spoke with Marc Bekoff, professor emeritus of ecology and evolutionary biology at the University of Colorado, about the handler-dog relationship. He was not surprised when I told him about Kevin Howard and his theory that dogs do not love their handlers. Bekoff reasoned that military handlers might adopt a psychological distancing mechanism because they know that by sending an animal to war, there is the danger that he will get hurt, maimed, or even killed. And this is when, he believes, the idea of loving this animal, and acknowledging that he loves you back, becomes very complicated.

When I asked Gutierrez to pinpoint what it was that cemented his relationship with Bert, he refrained from saying that "love" was a factor. So, I asked him, what would he call it? Bonding? Closeness? Affection?

"I guess you could say affection," he said. "But I think it's more of a 'I'm the pack leader, now you're going to listen to me.'"

But even after he credited Bert's bonding to the "wolf pack," Gutierrez said with a sheepish sigh, knowing that he was about to contradict all he had just said, "At the end of the day, you do grow attached and the dog knows it."

37

The day after Howard's no-love-for-the-working-dog speech, I went back out to Fort Carson. Jon Baer, a long-time friend of Jakubin's and a former Air Force handler, drove me there. He had been present when Howard spoke. Even though he hadn't said anything at the time, he told me that he believes there's a lot more to handler-dog dynamics than simply dominating a dog.

When a handler is assigned to a new home station, the first thing he works on with his dog is rapport building. Baer said that more important than establishing what handlers like Howard call the "alpha," this is a time to connect with the dog, to let the dog know how close they will be as partners. He took one hand off the wheel to cross his fingers, to make the sign of the closest of close together. Those beginning stages of training with a new dog are not the time, he said, to give a lot of corrections. Rather, it is the time to teach the dog to trust his handler.

These exercises were the very first thing Baer did as a military canine handler when he was partnered with his very first dog, Benny. Baer and Benny were a team for nearly three years, and Benny was Baer's favorite dog. "I loved that guy," he said. And then again, with more emphasis, "I *loved* that guy."

For each handler I talked to, there was always one dog who stood out, one dog who ranked above the others as uniquely special. And hearing about that dog was a lot like hearing someone talk about his first love. The favorite dog may or may not be the first dog, but there always *is* a favorite dog. And when a handler mentions this dog's name, there's a change in pitch in his voice and the inevitable smile that comes with remembering.

This is where all the talk about establishing the alpha or composing a mind-set where the dog is first and foremost viewed as a tool or a piece of equipment usually starts to veer off track. From everything I've seen, the closer a handler is with his dog, the better they perform.

Which brings me back to Jakubin and Taint and all the things he had told me about how he feels when the dogs die. It posed a disconnect that I simply could not wrap my mind around. Why couldn't something so plain just be called love?

Almost a year after our afternoon conversation at Fort Carson, I asked Jakubin the same question again. At first he gave me the same answer, but this time I argued with him. I pointed out that the ends don't meet: Their purpose and their training were distinctly at odds, this idea that the dog was a tool *and* a partner. That you were supposed to bond with the dog to elicit better results but still somehow remain unattached.

Jakubin talked around an answer for a few minutes, and I could tell he was getting frustrated. Whether he was annoyed with me or with the question, I didn't know, but he put an end to our discussion by telling me to e-mail him later on. He promised to send out my query to other handlers to see how they felt. So I did that, but he never posted the question. However, Jakubin himself e-mailed me after giving the idea more thought. His feelings, he wrote, were mixed:

A part of me says this is exactly how I feel and the other says this is totally opinionated based on each individual handler . . . it is definitely a controversial topic. Now you state, "you are not supposed to love your dog." Building that bond comes naturally. Me, I don't want to become attached but it just happens. I've cried every time I had to put a dog down. I couldn't really tell you if it was "love" or [because] the dog lived its entire life to give his life for me. . . . All in all there was some sort of attachment; handlers in general have trouble letting go . . . including me. With this being said I wouldn't have any trouble releasing my dog to protect me so I can go home to my family . . . that's the life of a police/war dog nothing more nothing less.

38

There's another point of view, one in which there is room both for love and for the utility of sacrifice implicit in an MWD's ultimate role in war. In fact, according to Lulofs, the most important tool you have as a handler is precisely the emotional bond you have with your dog. And that bond, he says, whether it's built in minutes or years, is necessary to having a successful dog. A dog, he says, has to trust his handler on an emotional level.

Lieutenant Colonel E. H. Richardson, the founder of the first British dog training school, trained World War I messenger dogs, and his techniques were used early on to train US war dogs. Richardson believed that trust was at the core of the relationship between a dog and his handler. He believed that virtually nothing could keep his messenger dogs from completing their task—not fatigue, not the temptation of food, not the call of a friendly soldier. As Richardson wrote, "It is safe to say, that if you can get a dog to understand a certain duty as a trust, it will rarely fail you. In fact, especially in relations to guarding duties, the dog will often rather lay down life itself than betray its trust."

Lt. Col. E. H. Richardson, "the father of war dogs" (at least as we know them today), pulls bandages from the kit of a British Red Cross dog, circa 1914.
Courtesy of the Library of Congress, Prints and Photographs Division

Bekoff believes that dogs have evolved over centuries to expect this special bond with humans, one they do not share with other species. And that expectation, he says, is hardwired into who they are. It is a shameful double cross to betray a dog, Bekoff says, because dogs implicitly and unquestioningly trust the humans with whom they bond.

Konrad Lorenz, a preeminent zoologist and Nobel Prize recipient, wrote extensively on the canine's ability to bond to his human companions and the responsibility that bond carries to the humans who make use of it. "The fidelity of a dog is a precious gift demanding no less binding moral responsibilities than the friendship of a human being. The bond with a true dog," he wrote in his very popular 1954 book *Man Meets Dog,* "is as lasting as the ties of this earth can ever be, a fact which should be noted by anyone who decides to acquire a canine friend."

Lulofs loved Aaslan, the dog who deployed with him to Iraq in 2004. And he has no trouble admitting it. But as much as he loved Aaslan, Lulofs has long since accepted the reality of the work he does, however harsh it might seem. The dogs go out in front, closest to the danger. It's the nature of the job, he says, to put your dog at risk. But, as a handler—who's next in line to danger—that's your job, too, to take slightly elevated risks.

When he was on patrol with the Marines in Iraq, Lulofs instructed them on what to do should he be critically wounded and Aaslan somehow made it impossible for them to help him. He told them to kill the dog "if the dog tries to defend me from everybody. My life is more important than my dog's. That dog is a dog. I will cry for him, but at the end of the day, he doesn't have a family, he doesn't have kids." For Lulofs, this is the one distinction that is absolute. "Even the softest, [most] cuddly handlers that I know," Lulofs said, understand whose life comes first.

But when bullets are coming and a handler's dog is out in the open and unprotected, this mentality doesn't always prevail. Handlers have gone to great lengths to protect and save their dogs.

39

It was the Fourth of July, 2011, in Afghanistan. Sometime around midnight, the wind kicked up an angry bluster around the base. A sandstorm swirled, drowning the sky. Darkness swallowed up the night. There was no visibility, not even the strongest light could cut across the impenetrable black. It meant a delay of the route clearance mission. For that, Army Specialist Marc Whittaker was glad.

Earlier in the evening, Whittaker had awoken with a bad feeling, a dread so strong that he wanted to refuse the assignment outright. But this, of course, was not an option. Still, the sandstorm filled him with a small hope. Maybe the whole mission would be scrubbed.

Whittaker and his explosive-detection dog Anax hadn't been stationed at Forward Operating Base (FOB) Shank in Logar Province for very long. The dog team had been on only a few missions since they arrived.

Anax had noticed the drag in Whittaker's mood and, though the three-year-old German shepherd wasn't prone to affection, he stayed close to his handler, nuzzling his head under Whittaker's hand. In a matter of hours the storm cleared, leaving behind gusty winds. The mission was back on.

By the time the sun made its entry into the sky and the temperature began its rapid climb, Whittaker's unit had been walking for miles. Whittaker started to sweat. Anax took the heat in stride and didn't show any signs of distress. They made it through the village to their destination without disturbance. The roads were quiet and seemingly empty. All was clear, and the resupply convoy got the okay to move ahead.

At the outpost, Whittaker, Anax, and the rest of their team of about 20 soldiers took a beat to catch their breath and rest in the shade, while they waited for the convoy to catch up. They'd been there only a few minutes when a call came in from a neighboring village that another unit had stumbled onto what they thought was an unexploded ordnance. Whittaker and Anax walked over with a Czech EOD team. It turned out to be a simple detonation, and the Czech team made fast work of disposing of the bomb.

By the time they returned to the outpost, the convoy had already made its drop-off and was ready for the return trip. The mission was nearly over.

Whittaker's team pulled their gear back on and headed toward the village. This time they chose an elevated path, an alleyway that ran high along the hillside and gave them a clear, downward view of the main road and the convoy. By now civilians were bustling about, busy with their early morning routines, getting to work, opening the shops, taking their children to school. Whittaker and Anax stuck to the center of the group as it spread out. Whittaker watched the first few convoy trucks roll along the road and then he heard an RPG explode, followed by the sound of gunfire. The convoy was being ambushed.

Whittaker heard orders come in loud over the radio. The unit was instructed to move from their position on the hillside into flanking maneuvers and to engage the enemy in an effort to draw the fire away from the convoy so it could make its way out of the village.

Everyone began to run fast down the hill over low walls and ditches. They raced through the twisted alleys, closing the distance to the convoy. Whittaker had his hands on his weapon while Anax, still hooked to his side on the retractable leash, kept pace beside him. The dog was just as amped as the rest of them. He fed off their anxiety and adrenaline but didn't make a sound, not a bark or a whimper.

The locals they passed were unfazed by the barrage of bullets and assault weapons. A man rode by on his bike. It was as if they were operating on another plane of existence. The sounds of war had become so commonplace they were only background noises here, like the ringing of church bells.

Whittaker and Anax continued to run, feet and paws pounding on the ground, and neared a wall, the final obstacle between them and the road. Bullets ricocheted off houses, echoing throughout the valley, which made it impossible to determine the enemy's position. They jumped the four-foot drop to the road and landed right in the line of fire.

When bullets make a whizzing noise, you know they're close. When you can hear them cracking, they're even closer. As soon as Whittaker and Anax hit the ground, the sound of cracking flooded Whittaker's ears. He and Anax were stuck, pinned down in the wide-open middle of the road.

Without his body armor, Anax was exposed, and Whittaker instinctively threw himself across the dog, using his own body as a shield. If bullets were to hit them, they would hit his vest. But Anax squirmed under his weight, fighting his hold. Anax snapped his jaws at nothing, at everything, and finally made contact, sinking his teeth into Whittaker's hand, three of his sharp teeth piercing through Whittaker's glove and skin. Anax's jaw had closed in a full-mouth bite around the whole of Whittaker's hand, near his thumb and down around his pinky finger. But in the heat of the commotion, Whittaker barely registered the sensation.

The barrage lasted two full minutes. Then the air shifted and Whittaker noticed the shots sounded different. Now it was his guys who were laying down suppressive fire. If they were going to move, they had to move now. He pushed himself up off the ground, ready to run, but his dog, who was always out ahead, wasn't moving. Whittaker glanced back and saw that Anax's eyes were open. He looked as if he wanted to follow but he couldn't. He was frozen. And that's when Whittaker knew something was very wrong.

He grabbed Anax by the collar and, giving up hope of reaching the others, dragged the dog to the nearest cover, a solid wall just a few feet away. Whittaker's hands flew along the dog's body, assessing him from head to tail. The dog was breathing, but he was whining and twisting in pain. And then Whittaker saw the blood on Anax's hind legs.

Fear set in. Whittaker didn't have Anax's medical kit with him. He'd left it on the truck, which was still over at the dismount site. He pulled the bandages from his own medical kit and pressed gauze to Anax's wound to try to stem the bleeding. *This can't be happening. This can't be happening.* The thought hurtled through his mind again and again.

By that point, an air weapons team had been called in, and the firefight was basically over. Whittaker finished wrapping the gauze around Anax's leg as best he could. A lieutenant got on the radio to let command know they needed an IV for Anax as well as a helicopter to get him to treatment.

But the medic was occupied treating a civilian contractor from the convoy who had sustained a head injury when it was attacked. A medevac had already been called for the injured man and was on its way to the dismount site. If they could get there in time, the medevac would transport Anax to a hospital.

The site was a mile and a half away.

Whittaker took Anax in his arms and heaved him up, cradling the dog. He tried for one short, stilted step and then another, but as he trudged forward, he could feel the dog's fur slide from his grip. The pair nearly dropped to the ground. Anax was 80 pounds of dead weight in his arms. They had been out in the hot sun for hours and had already walked for miles. Whittaker was drenched in sweat. He was so exhausted he could not carry his dog more than a few feet.

The Czech EOD guys who had stayed with Whittaker and his wounded dog rushed to help. After stripping off their shirts, they tied the fabric together into a bridge of cloth. Together they pulled the dog up, but with his wriggling and writhing, he kept slipping out of the makeshift stretcher, which greatly slowed their efforts.

Whittaker's panic was now full blown. They weren't going to make it to the medevac. Anax's eyes were glazing over, his gaze was distant. The dog was about to go into shock. Even if they made it back to the dismount site, he knew that the medical kit alone wouldn't be enough now. Anax needed emergency care.

Whittaker shouted at the lieutenant, "I need to get my dog on that bird! We have to get on that bird!" He yelled it again and again.

Then Whittaker heard the sound of a truck. It was an Afghan local. Whittaker heard the voices, the sounds of negotiation. The EOD guys managed to communicate the urgency of the situation, and the Afghan man agreed to lend them his truck. They piled in. There was the blur of movement, the jolt of the rocky road beneath them. They were moving, they were moving.

When they pulled up to the medevac site, the signal smoke that marked its spot was already billowing high in the air. Within minutes, the helicopter was on the ground.

They had made it.

Anax would lose one of his right legs, but he would survive.

40

Human feelings for dogs can run deep. Canine feelings, it turns out, can actually be quite complex as well. Dogs, in fact, have a startling emotional intelligence, especially when they relate to humans.

In 2006, Dr. Juliane Kaminski, a cognitive psychologist at the Max Planck Institute for Evolutionary Anthropology in Germany, conducted a study that sought to compare "the use of causal and communicative cues in an object choice task" between dogs and chimpanzees. Footage taken of the same kinds of trials conducted during this study shows Dr. Kaminski at the Leipzig Zoo facing a chimpanzee. There is a plastic divide between them as well as a table. On the table two banana-yellow cups are turned over, bottoms up. The objective is for the chimp to reach through two circular holes in the divide and find the food hidden beneath one of these cups.

Dr. Kaminski is there to help. She points to the cup containing the food. Her signals offer reliable and consistent information. All the chimp has to do is watch Dr. Kaminski and follow her movements, and she will find the food. Only she doesn't. The sweet face, with its deep wrinkles framed in wispy black hairs, hardly turns in the direction of Kaminski, even as the doctor speaks directly to her, conveying not just words but emotions, with her face as well as her hands. Each time the experiment is repeated, the chimp continues to make her own choices without acknowledging Kaminski's exaggerated gestures, often making her choice before the doctor even attempts to point out the food.

During another test, Kaminski is in a different room, and this time there isn't a plastic wall or a table, just two overturned blue bowls on the floor. The experiment is the same, only now she is standing in front of a dog. From the moment the exercise begins, the dog's eyes are trained on her face. And this time, when Kaminski points to the food, the dog's response is immediate. He moves directly to the blue bowl that she indicated, and he finds the food.

The dog used Kaminski's direction—what she calls "informed" gestures—while the chimpanzee did not. This experiment shows, she says, that the communication between human and canine is "in its essence a very cooperative interaction." For dogs, this kind of "following, pointing seems to be very natural, and it makes dogs extremely interesting." It is proof, she believes, of their extraordinary social intelligence, a grasping of something akin to a second language. They've learned "to interpret human communication, which is different from dog communication."

Further evidence shows that dogs have the ability not only to read and register our gestures, but also to interpret the emotional expressions on our faces. At the University of Lincoln in England, Daniel Mills, professor of veterinary behavioral medicine, conducted a study using eye-tracking technology to better understand how dogs and humans interact with each other.

Humans reveal emotions more prominently on the right side of our faces. This means that when we talk to each other, whether we realize it or not, we gaze left at the faces of our friends and others in order to best assess their mood.

With this in mind, Mills set up his experiment by placing dogs in front of a screen onto which he projected images of human faces. Some were smiling or frowning, while others showed no expression. Mills then used eye-tracking technology to determine what the dog's eyes looked at, to determine if they looked at human expression at all. It turns out, as Mills discovered, that dogs also gaze left. They seek out the right side of the human face, the "emotional" side. His findings provide strong evidence to support the idea that dogs read human expression, that they knowingly look and then decipher information from our faces.

But though these experiments show that dogs are uniquely in tune with humans and human emotions, they do not "prove" the existence of love. And for the most part, the study of the beneficial effects of the emotional exchange between man and dog has largely been one-sided. There have been quite a few scientific studies about what dogs do for humans. For instance, we know their company lowers our blood pressure and greatly reduces the stress we feel. But there have been few studies on the positive effect of humans on dogs.

One study that *did* examine the effect of the canine-human bond on both dogs and humans centered on oxytocin, which is best known as the mammalian hormone of love. In 2010, researchers at the Karolinska Institutet in Sweden presented a study that looked at levels of oxytocin when dogs and humans were together. What the study found is that after a "petting session" with their dog, the dog's owner experienced a boost in his level of oxytocin. Perhaps even more interesting than the appearance of oxytocin in blood samples of the human subjects was that a similar spike in the hormone was seen in the blood samples taken from the dogs. This finding supports the idea that the bonding emotions really do go both ways.

Still, Bekoff readily concedes that there is a lack of focus on *proving* the bond. The evidence is still largely anecdotal. But then, he wonders, do we really need such studies? The reason they don't exist, he believes, is because we don't need them. The idea is backed by something far simpler—common sense.

He poses it this way. "If you define love as an enduring and a strong bond—I love you, I miss you, I seek you out, I prefer you," why, he asks, can't this be transferred to the dog? In other words, *of course* dogs love us.

41

One day I followed Jakubin into the back of the USAF Academy kennels where each dog has his own separate quarters, a space of six feet by six feet, walled on all four sides by chain-link fence. As soon as Jakubin opened the door, a commotion erupted, and all the dogs were up on their feet. Some wagged their tails, clearly happy to see him. They took little note of my presence, all except for Boda, who, as soon as I set foot near her house, made it clear that I was an intruder, unwelcome and unwanted. She barked sharply and loudly in my direction. Her growls became more beastly the closer I got.

Boda was one of Jakubin's misfit cases. She had arrived at the kennels with a superior detection record, but once they took her outside a controlled training-yard environment, her nerves began to show. Unexpected noises and unknown objects frightened her, and she shied from crowds, cowering in chaotic parking lots. Jakubin knew there was no way he could send this dog out on a deployment without a tremendous amount of work. So they were gradually trying to build up her confidence, trying to alleviate her fears.

One afternoon, while we were sitting outside at Fort Carson, I watched as Boda's handler, Staff Sergeant Robbie Whaley, ran a metal brush through her thick coat, sending tufts of fur into the air, like dandelion seeds. Boda's velvety ears sank with pleasure. Whaley, in the midst of this focused caregiving, had overheard the chatter about handlers loving or not loving their dogs but had chosen not to participate. Whatever had been said did not deter him from planting a kiss on Boda's muzzle, a kiss she accepted without flinching.

When the grooming finally ceased, Boda turned her head in my direction. I wanted her to trust me, so I offered the very same gesture my father taught me at a young age, when he cautioned me, "Never force your hand on a dog." I rested my elbows on my knees and extended my open hands, palms to the sky.

Boda finally approached me, ever careful as she took a sniff of and then gave a lick to first my left hand, then my right. I didn't touch her or speak. She hovered and then pushed her large face close to mine. I could feel her nose cold on my cheek. I got a lick before she bounced back over to Whaley. Then a few moments later, she returned, her large nose sniffing my hair so close I could smell the cold air fresh on her coat. This time I didn't hesitate to catch the scruff of her neck and reach up behind her ears to give them a good scratch. She leaned into my hand and settled against me on the ground. I could feel her heaviness, her warmth. It was a peaceful exchange, quiet and complete. I had been accepted. I was a friend.

A little while later Boda, emboldened by her shining coat, sashayed around the group of us, weaving in and out of our circle, a pull toy in her mouth. The other handlers called to her, reaching out their hands to engage her in a game of tug-of-war. She heard them but ultimately denied them all, coming close but not close enough. At last she brought the toy to her handler—and only her handler. She placed it at Whaley's feet.

Whaley looked down at her and smiled. He was convinced that this dog loved him. She, in turn, regarded him, waiting and watching. The expression on her face was a mix of expectation and adoration. This was a face inviting play, and she had clearly chosen her playmate.

42

In many ways, military dogs are trained to be brave. They're exposed to rifle fire, machine gun fire, and the sound of explosions. They learn to navigate underground tunnels, climb ladders, and even scale walls. "The War Dog," Richardson wrote, "has to have all fear of explosions and firing, smoke clouds, water obstacles etc. eliminated." But he also felt that the behavior in dogs that drove them to exceed even the highest expectations and, say, cover their handlers' bodies during an attack was an impulse of their intrinsic character, and a distinctly canine sensibility. "Apart from this trained courage," he continued, "we can all recall instances of natural pluck and real bravery in dogs, defending some person, or thing they valued, and believed to be in danger."

It was an instinct that Richardson believed an adept handler might pull out of the dog during training, but not one that every dog possessed or even could be trained to feel.

There is a rich history of military service dogs not only showing love but also being willing to protect and defend human life, even at their own expense.

Military service dogs began to edge their way into the war-front headlines during World War I. In October 1917, Mrs. Euphistone Maitland, secretary of the Blue Cross, told the *New York Times* about the heroics of the dogs in the trenches, their unflappable will to work, and their ability to pick the wounded men from the dead. "They know their men," she said, "and possess an instinctive love for them." Each dog, in her mind, had a favorite soldier for whom he showed preference. "Dogs," she said, "have been known to shield wounded men and so save the lives of the soldiers at the loss of their own."

During World War II, the Associated Press sent out a dispatch from the island of Guam about one of the Marine Corps' trained "battle-hardened devil dogs," a Doberman named Lucky. After a successful mission to uncover Japanese snipers, Lucky was "found crouched close to his wounded handler in a gully near a concrete bridge over Asan River. . . . When the marines started to give first-aid to the wounded handler Lucky growled. But he let them work on his master. When the latter died Lucky moved to the side of the body and would not permit any to approach." The sergeant who finally had to pull the dog away with what the paper described as a "noose" said, "That's the way these war dogs are—one man dogs."

On a December night in 1966, while patrolling a cemetery with his dog Nemo just inside Son Nhut Air Base near Saigon, handler Robert Thorneburg, an airman second class, was attacked by Vietcong still hiding on the grounds.

Thorneburg sent Nemo to give chase, and the dog ran off ahead. The sound of shots rang out, quickly followed by Nemo's yelps. The dog had taken a bullet to the face, and as the firefight continued, Thorneburg was also hit. Despite his injury, Nemo found his handler and maneuvered himself on top of Thorneburg. Nemo guarded Thorneburg until help came. Nemo lost an eye, but both dog and handler survived the attack.

Nearly 45 years later, a black Labrador retriever named Eli shielded his young Marine handler, Colton Rusk, in exactly the same way during a firefight with the Taliban.

Both at the beginning of their military careers, Rusk and Eli were inseparable, and they both appeared playful and fresh-faced, dark and handsome.

They had been in Afghanistan for only a few months when, on December 6, 2010, Rusk was hit by Taliban sniper fire. He fell where he stood. As the bullets continued to fly, Eli crawled on top of him. When the other Marines rushed to Rusk's aid, Eli snapped at them. He refused to allow anyone to breach his protection. He even bit one of the other men to keep him from touching Rusk. The other Marines were able to distract the dog away from Rusk's body without harm coming to anyone else. Unfortunately, however, nothing could be done. Private First Class Rusk died that same day.

43

As the sun descended in Afghanistan on a June day in 2011, the desert air began to cool. The night would be clear and offer good visibility. There was nothing remarkable about the smell of the coming night air, nor the feel of his gear, thought Staff Sergeant John Mariana as he pulled on his Kevlar vest, just as he'd done time and time before. He looked down at Bronco, taking in the top of the dog's head with its marble-rye blacks and browns. The dog looked up, returning his gaze with the dark eyes Mariana had found so reassuring during their eight months in Afghanistan.

By this time, Mariana and Bronco had carved out a well-honed pre-mission ritual. Mariana began by giving the eight-year-old Belgian Malinois an IV drip. The fluids would keep Bronco well hydrated during long missions. When the drip was finished, Mariana ran Bronco through a few quick explosive-odor recognition drills, just enough to get the dog clicked into a working mind-set. Finally, Mariana took hold of his weapon and sat with Bronco on the ground, where they waited together until it was time to go. This was the way they found their meditative calm before the storm of combat.

That night Mariana and Bronco waited for the mission to begin, along with the SF team they'd been with since November. Typically, dog teams are not assigned to a single unit for any extended period of time. They operate more like moonlighters, setting out from their main station for short stints on smaller patrol bases and joining up with units for mission-specific operations. When a handler and his dog are assigned to work with SF, it's a trial by fire, and the window for a handler to prove himself and the worth of his dog is open for only a short time.

Mariana looked like an SF guy, tall and brawny, with a sleeve tattoo wrapping the length of his right arm. During the months of their deployment, his dark hair had grown out to match the beard on his face, as full and thick as the sound of his New York accent. A thrill seeker, he was up for anything. On their first night with their new team, Mariana and Bronco had uncovered four explosives, three of them IEDs. They'd been with the same SF guys ever since, putting some 80 missions behind them.

Under the cover of dark, the team began the first leg of their mission. As usual, Mariana and Bronco took the lead, working out in front of the rest of the patrol. Bronco searched ahead off leash. They'd been moving steadily for about an hour and had entered a village. Mariana took off his NVGs, as he often did on a night like this one. He preferred to let his eyes adjust to the natural dark in case he was forced to rely on his own vision.

When they neared the first objective of their mission, Mariana clipped Bronco back onto the leash at his waist to keep him close. Fully engrossed in his sniffing, Bronco had his head low to the ground. Mariana locked a careful eye on his dog, waiting, watching for the signal that Bronco was on odor. Suddenly there was a man standing just 10 feet in front of them, which caught Mariana completely by surprise. And the man was pointing an AK-47 straight at him.

The command that sent Bronco to attack burst from Mariana in pure reflex, as he popped the leash and freed the dog from his side. Bronco bolted forward toward their attacker and Mariana raised his flashlight to flood the man's face with blinding white light. The dog cleared the short distance between them and caught the man's upper torso with a strong bite. There was a blur of limbs and fur, but Bronco's teeth held their grip. The man struggled to fight off the 65 pounds of dog that'd just attacked him. Then Mariana saw the barrel of the rifle flash down toward Bronco's head.

A gunshot rang out. A single round was fired. Then everything that had been happening entirely too fast for Mariana to comprehend began to slow and pass before his eyes in freeze frame. Mariana could see the force of the bullet as it hit Bronco. He watched the dog's head shake in a slow-wrenching wave.

As soon as the ring of the gunshot was over, time caught back up to tempo. There was a rush of movement as the scene around Mariana erupted in chaos. Within moments their attacker was no longer a threat. But Bronco had disappeared.

Mariana's mind raced. Bronco had run off, but whether in pain or in fear he couldn't be sure. He was certain Bronco had just taken a bullet to the head. There was blood splashed on the ground. Along with another soldier, Mariana rushed to follow the dark-spotted trail. His heart thudded and adrenaline pulsed through his muscles, as his thoughts ramped up into panic.

The men moved quickly. Mariana called out for Bronco. After a few yards the trail started to thin, becoming more difficult to see. If Bronco was still alive, his wound would likely be hemorrhaging blood. There'd be no way the dog could survive it. Then, about 100 yards out, the two men rounded the corner of a building and there was Bronco, sitting quiet and still. He was covered in blood but sitting all the same, waiting for his handler as if it had been the plan to rally at this safe spot all along. Mariana flew to him and inspected the wound. Bronco had been hit in the face. The bullet had entered the left side of his mouth and had traveled straight through, virtually dissolving the right side of the dog's muzzle. It shattered the bone in the front part of his nose and fractured the teeth along his upper jaw.

They called in a medevac. Mariana pressed gauze to the wound, and each cloth too quickly absorbed blood. The bullet had done something to obstruct the dog's nasal passages, and Bronco was having trouble breathing. He began to sneeze over and over. With each sneeze came a new spray of blood as the force of air burst the clot that had just congealed. Though Mariana did his best to stop the bleeding around the wound, he realized there was little he could do. Bronco needed to breathe through his wound. Covering it would suffocate him. Mariana could only mop up the blood.

After more than a few minutes of this, Bronco slumped to the ground, sprawled over on his side. Mariana's heart stopped. He stared hard into the dog's eyes, and then a terrible kind of relief washed over Mariana as he realized Bronco hadn't just bled out in front of him. Instead, he had rolled over to offer his belly up for a scratch. Mariana exhaled, marveling at the strength of his dog.

But the lifted feeling was only temporary, and guilt soon took hold. He pulled Bronco into his arms and leaned down over the dog's ear. "I'm sorry, buddy," he whispered. "I'm sorry." With one hand he massaged the inside of Bronco's ear, the way the dog liked it, trying to soothe and comfort him, trying to reassure him that he was safe. "If we make it through this," Mariana whispered, "if we make it home, I'm going to take care of you."

It seemed like hours, but within 45 minutes they were in the medevac. As they moved across the sky, Mariana allowed himself to catch his breath for the first time that night. He looked up. The stars were so bountiful and so bright and they felt too close, like the lights of some floating aerial metropolis.

By the time they reached Kandahar almost another hour later, the first rays of morning light were showing. The medevac descended, but there wasn't an ambulance on the ground standing by as had been promised over the radio. Mariana scanned the area, but there was neither sight nor sound of an approaching engine. No one was waiting for them, and as far as he could see, no one was coming.

Mariana wasn't going to wait. He pulled Bronco from the floor of the helicopter, hoisted the dog over his shoulders, and began the roughly 300-yard stretch from the landing site to the hospital on foot. Bronco rode along uncomplainingly, his furry side pressing heavily into the back of Mariana's neck. Exhausted, Mariana felt that, at best, his speed registered no faster than a walk. But in fact he was running with all the strength he had left.

When they reached Kandahar's main hospital, the staff inside the front door took Bronco and sent him on a stretcher to emergency surgery. However, they refused to let Mariana, who was still wearing his weapon, stay inside. Furious and frantic, he went back outside, pulled off his Kevlar, and threw it on the ground. He was forced to wait. He didn't sleep. He didn't eat. A friend came to keep him company. Though he rarely smoked, Mariana burned through almost an entire pack of cigarettes. Nothing helped.

Five hours later, the doctors finally delivered a groggy Bronco from surgery. The dog was in stable condition and the prognosis was positive. Still, they could do only so much for Bronco at the human hospital. They were going to transport Mariana and Bronco from Kandahar back to Bagram, one of the largest US bases in Afghanistan, where the veterinary technicians were stationed. Mariana asked for some blankets and set up a bed on the floor. Bronco's nose was so swollen that he was barely able to breathe. Mariana lay on the floor with him, took the dog's head onto his chest, and held the dog's mouth open so he could get more air.

When they finally got to Bagram, Mariana was still wearing his bloodied clothes. He'd left everything of his own behind. The only things he had carried out of that night mission—gauze, IVs, toys, water—had been for Bronco.

Marine IEDD Chaney mugs for the camera.
Courtesy of Corporal Matt Hatala

Lance Corporal Trevor M. Smith, a Marine dog handler, taunts Grek, a combat tracker dog, who replies with intimidating snarls while they train together at Combat Outpost Rawah, Iraq, on December 3, 2008.

Photo by Lance Corporal Sean Cummins

MWD Dyngo takes a break in the shade after he and his former handler Tech Sergeant Justin Kitts ran through an obstacle course at the Department of Defense K-9 Trials at Lackland Air Force Base in Texas on May 5, 2012. Dyngo and Kitts deployed to Afghanistan together in 2011.

US Air Force Staff Sergeant Joshua Fehringer guides MWD Suk across the obedience course at Cannon Air Force Base in New Mexico on August 15, 2012.

Photo by Airman First Class Xavier Lockley

IEDD Molly keeps Seaman James L. Louck company at a new Afghan Uniformed Police security post in the village of Regay, in Musa Qal'eh district, Helmand Province, Afghanistan on February 1, 2012.

Photo by Sergeant Earnest J. Barnes

Staff Sergeant Pascual Gutierrez carries his dog, Mack, down a hill at Lackland Air Force Base in May 2012.

Staff Sergeant Robbie Whaley plays with MWD Boda after giving her a good grooming at Fort Carson in Colorado in December 2011.

MWD Turbo stands with his handler during a training exercise at Yuma Proving Ground in March 2012.

While on foot patrol a group of Marines found Layla (above) when she was a puppy, but because of IED risk, taking her on patrols was too dangerous, and they decided to trade her for some cigars to the Marines of the 1st Battalion, 8th Infantry Regiment. Here she is with her Marines from the 1/8 at Shir Ghazay Patrol Base in Landay Nawah County, Afghanistan.

© Rita Leistner/Basetrack

Layla relaxes in the arms of one of the Marines who took her in during their deployment to Afghanistan.

© *Rita Leistner/Basetrack*

Marine Sergeant Charlie Hardesty works with MWD Turbo during a training session at YPG.

US Air Force MWD Luck goes through an obstacle course on March 8, 2010, at Hurlburt Field in Florida.

Photo by Staff Sergeant Sheila Devera

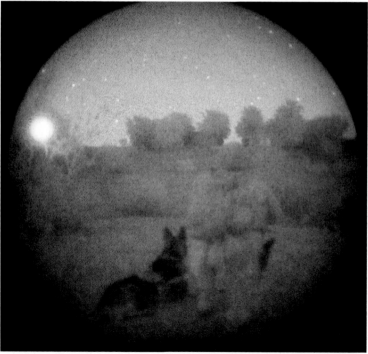

Marine Lance Corporal Joshua Ashley takes a knee with MWD Sirius during a nighttime training exercise at YPG in March 2012.

Combat Tracker dog Lex—who loves attention—enjoys some free time with his handler, Marine Lance Corporal John Peeler.

44

In the two weeks that followed, Bronco underwent two additional reconstructive surgeries in an attempt to repair the damage. Sections of his nose had to be removed and replaced.

While they were in Bagram, Mariana never left Bronco's side. He listened to his shifting, choppy breathing, always with one hand on the dog's mouth to keep the airway open. But even that wasn't enough. Within a few weeks, Bronco and Mariana were sent back to the States, to the hospital at Lackland Air Force Base, for more surgery. And, soon after they returned from Afghanistan, the two were separated.

The time apart from the dog who had saved his life wore on him, and Mariana dealt with it terribly. He was tormented with thoughts of bad, wicked things. It didn't matter that he was back at his home station and back with his family or that his wife was about to have a baby. He wanted to be with Bronco. Mariana was losing sight of himself.

It was a long time before Mariana saw Bronco again. The dog wasn't able to do detection work anymore and would be retiring from service. Mariana had to fight to get the dog back, and even with the support of higher-ups, it wasn't easy. The battle spanned five long months. On the day they were reunited, the effect was instantaneous: Mariana felt the weight break and fall away like the cracking of a glacial crust of ice. He saw Bronco in the kennel and grabbed his dog, crying freely.

In his joyful frenzy at seeing his handler, Bronco's nose, which would never be quite the same again, whistled like a teakettle.

When Mariana talked about Bronco, he was adamant that the strength of their working relationship was based on a mutual commitment and a deep and shared connection. "He didn't work for me out of fear of me correcting him. He worked for me because he loved me and I loved him. And I really believe that he knew that."

A loving dog makes for a formidable asset in war.

45

The day Marine Lance Corporal Matt Hatala was paired up with Chaney, his new IED detector dog and soon-to-be deployment partner, he went home frustrated, utterly convinced there was no way he could work with this dog. Chaney had been paired with another handler and wanted nothing to do with this new Marine. The black Labrador retriever was 85 pounds of strong-willed stubbornness, and though he never became aggressive or mean, the dog simply refused to listen to Hatala, and used his weight to cement his resistance.

Chaney may have been heavy—literally hard to lift—but Hatala, who was strong and agile after his years of high school wrestling, could handle the dog's size. And with patience, he was able to weather the dog's attitude. Slowly, steadily, over the next couple of months of training, Chaney became more trusting of Hatala. By the time they deployed to Afghanistan's southern Helmand Province in October 2010, they were finally in sync.

Hatala and Chaney were stationed at Patrol Base Tar, a small military outpost named for a detection dog who had been killed there by an IED and who had saved the lives of three men on patrol in the process. There were only about eight Marines at Tar, and a couple of Afghan National Army soldiers. At night the Marines bunked in a mud hut. At first Hatala kept Chaney's kennel outside, insulating it as best he could by tucking hay around the bottom and wrapping a poncho around it. But the temperatures began to drop, and Chaney was soon sleeping inside, tied to Hatala's cot. After a while, trusting that Chaney would stay where he was supposed to, Hatala let him off the leash.

Every morning as soon as he woke up, Hatala would take Chaney outside to do his business. It was always early, and most times they would catch the sun rising over the desert. It was Hatala's favorite time of day, calm and quiet. He would watch his dog and listen to the music his wife had burned onto CDs for him and sent over, letting the sound of it flood his ears. Hatala was growing very attached to Chaney. The dog had become his anchor, his best friend. The other guys loved Chaney, too, and though it went against his training, Hatala never felt it was right to keep them from petting his dog. Why should he be the only one to benefit from Chaney's good company? They all had tough days, and Chaney was especially good at picking out who among their unit was in the darkest mood. The dog would seek out whoever it was and just nuzzle up next to him.

The Marines at the base took part in daily morning, afternoon, and night patrols, traveling back and forth between the nearby town and the base, ensuring that their area of operation was secure and checking in with locals. Their small base was mostly surrounded by desert that was flecked with small farms. Farther out, about a third of a mile from the back of their compound, was a small town settled into an embankment. Houses lined the top and bottom of the ridge. Beyond that, there was only wide-open nothingness that stretched until a mountain range.

The Marines had relatively good relations with the Afghans who lived there. The only things that interrupted their missions were the massive Afghan dogs who would alert to their otherwise discreet nighttime presence. These outside dogs were large and unruly and never tied up. At night they roamed around in packs. Hatala and his unit often heard them at the back of the base rummaging through the garbage.

On one afternoon patrol, Hatala, Chaney, and a few others were making their way through the town on the low side of the ridge. The patrol was spread out, their interpreter was in the middle, and Chaney was working off leash while Hatala and his friend, Lance Corporal Shea Boland, were out in front. Up ahead, Hatala spied one of the yard hounds stalking toward them. The dog was well over 100 pounds, his coat a tangled mess of gray, his white underbelly and legs caked in dirt. The dog's back was arched, and he was growling. They'd crossed into whatever this dog considered his territory, and he was coming straight for Boland.

The soldiers weren't authorized to shoot these dogs, so Boland threw a rock at him to scare him off. The dog, however, showed no sign of fear, and only skulked closer. A few feet behind Boland, Hatala readied himself to shoot if the dog attacked his friend. And then Chaney came out of nowhere and planted himself in front of Boland. His hackles were raised, and his muzzle was quivering. He let out a deep, savage growl. When the giant dog moved, Chaney moved to block him. He didn't allow the other dog to get any closer.

Keeping one eye on Chaney, Hatala motioned to Boland and the others, and they slowly moved the patrol forward and away from the yard dog. Chaney stood his ground, snarling, his body always between this threat and the other men.

When they were finally clear, Hatala called out, "Hey, hey. Chaney, here!" Chaney broke the standoff and trotted to rejoin his handler. The other dog watched them for a while and then lost interest.

Until that day, Hatala had never heard Chaney growl. Not once. Hatala had only heard him bark once or twice in all the months that they were together. That afternoon was the first and only time Hatala ever saw Chaney show aggression of any kind. He'd revealed himself to be a dog to be reckoned with.

part four

the fallen

If there are no dogs in heaven, then when I die I want to go where they went.

—Will Rogers

46

Lance Corporal Joshua Ashley arrived in Afghanistan in May 2012, two months after he finished his stint at the ISAK course at YPG in Arizona.

He wasn't the only handler from the II Marines Expeditionary Force (II-MEF) to deploy to Afghanistan, but the teams were assigned to different units. In mid-July, a few of them crossed paths at Camp Leatherneck. They sat around the same fire, smoking Cuban cigars and catching up, sharing their stories. Ashley talked about how much he loved deployment, how satisfying it was because he was doing what he came to do. He'd already signed up for reenlistment.

It was the last time the guys from II-MEF would see him alive.

On the night of July 18, 2012, Ashley and Sirius, assigned to a Marine Corps Forces Special Operations Command (MARSOC) unit, were patrolling along the Helmand River. Ashley was following Sirius, wading through a canal, when he stepped onto a pressure plate and set off an IED. The force of the explosion blew him backward. His unit called a medevac and cleared the area as quickly as they could. They managed to get Ashley to Camp Leatherneck, but he died the following day.

Ashley's was not the first fatality handlers from II-MEF had endured that summer. Just two days earlier, Lance Corporal Kent Ferrell and his Patrol Explosives Detection Dog Zora, a German shepherd, were out on a foot patrol. Zora was walking ahead of her handler and the combat engineer who was with them as she and Ferrell cleared an alley. A grenade sailed over the wall like a bird, and they watched as it landed on the ground in front of them. The engineer veered sharply and started to run. Ferrell yelled for Zora. She came toward him, but the grenade exploded. Shrapnel went flying. A shard struck the engineer in the elbow, but Zora, caught between the engineer and the explosion, absorbed the brunt of it. She took one piece to the neck, two to her face, and two directly to her chest. When Zora reached Ferrell a few moments later, she lay down next to him and died. It took less than a minute for her to go. The vet who performed the necropsy at Camp Leatherneck said a piece of shrapnel had nicked Zora's heart. Even if the vet had been there the moment it happened, there would have been nothing he or anyone else could have done to save her.

Ferrell had traveled back to Camp Leatherneck with Zora. He was there when they brought Ashley in to try to save him. And that is how Ferrell, who had just lost his dog, became the surrogate caretaker to Sirius, the dog who had just lost his handler.

As the flight crew prepared for takeoff on the C-130 that would deliver Ashley's body back to his family in the States, Ferrell and Sirius stood together on the tarmac. A crowd of servicemen and women came to pay their respects.

It was quiet, unearthly quiet for an airfield. It was apparent to those present that Sirius was in distress. And when the ramp ceremony finished and Ashley's body was boarded onto the aircraft, Sirius kept turning back to look at the plane.

47

The year 2012 was an especially brutal year for the MWD community. The losses had started in April of that year and continued through the summer, almost without pause.

On April 12, Marine Lance Corporal Abraham Tarwoe was killed in action. Two weeks later on April 26, Army Staff Sergeant Dick A. Lee Jr. was killed in action. In May, two handlers were killed "during combat operations." Marine Corporal Keaton Coffey died on May 24, and, six days later, on May 30, Navy handler Petty Officer Second Class Sean Brazas was shot in Panjwai, Afghanistan. There was a brief respite in June, and then Ashley died on July 19. Two days later, on July 21, Petty Officer Second Class Michael J. Brodsky succumbed to the injuries he sustained from an IED blast on July 7.

During those same months, MWDs Fibi, Zora, Nina, and Paco were all killed in action in Afghanistan. There were also canine wounded. Layka, a Belgian Malinois Air Force dog, lost her leg after being shot protecting her handler. JaJo, a German shepherd and part of the Army's Tactical Explosive Detection Dog (TEDD) program, was seriously wounded along with his handler by an IED explosion during a ground patrol on September 15. And then there were the dogs and handlers who made it back, whole in body but not so in spirit.

For the most part, when it comes to K-9, it doesn't seem to matter what branch handlers serve, they're all part of the same community, and in a combat theater, they are all searching for the same bombs. Word of injuries and death travels quickly.

It was Kitts who called to tell me that Ashley had been killed. "We lost another handler," he told me. "You know this one." Ashley had been Kitts's favorite student. Three days later, Kitts again delivered bad news. He texted me to tell me that Brodsky had died. "Three students in three months," Kitts wrote. "How many more friends do I have to lose?"

When Hardesty heard about Ashley's and then Brodsky's deaths, he was teaching at Yuma, running a new class of handlers through tactical drills, getting them ready to go on deployments. He texted me to make sure I had heard the news about Brodsky. I replied that I had and asked him how he was holding up. "Praying for a better tomorrow," he wrote back.

One night during that summer, while Hardesty and I talked on the phone, I asked him if he'd lost very many friends to these wars. He said that he felt lucky. He had known quite a few people who had been injured, some of them pretty badly, but, he said, he hadn't lost a lot of people close to him.

"But," Hardesty clarified, "I guess that depends on what you think of as 'a lot.'"

I told him that one sounded like a lot to me. "Well, then it's been a lot." He kind of laughed as he said this, but the sound was sad.

News of the losses was hard for all the Yuma instructors. The only slight consolation was that no one had died because they had failed to learn and apply the lessons of their training. One thing ISAK can't teach, though, is how to dodge bullets.

48

July 31, 2011, was Army Veterinary Specialist William Vidal's second night in Afghanistan. He'd barely been in-country 48 hours with the Army's 64th Medical Detachment (Veterinary Services) when someone knocked at his door. The voice on the other side told him to get ready, that a body was coming. Vidal roused and dressed. He had known going in that this was part of the job, but his very first act in Afghanistan would not be as a healer but as an undertaker.

Earlier that night, three MARSOC Marines stationed in western Afghanistan had died in a fire that had started in their living quarters and quickly burned out of control. The bodies were brought to Bagram Airfield by plane. There were enough servicemen on hand to give the fallen Marines honors, so the group formed a line and passed the bodies, as they came off the plane, from one set of hands to the next. Each of the litters that came off the plane was draped in an American flag. One litter held a body that was clearly much smaller than the rest. Vidal and Captain Katie Barry and Sergeant Alyssa Doughty, also of the 64th, placed the smallest body bag in their truck as some of the soldiers and airmen gave a final salute to their fallen comrade: Tosca, a Belgian Malinois who had died in the fire alongside her handler, Marine Sergeant Christopher Wrinkle.

The veterinary team brought Tosca's body into the examining room and opened the bag. Vidal could barely tell that what was on the table in front of them had once been a dog.

Tosca's distinguishing features had been all but erased. Only her collar remained intact. Barry removed it before they zipped the bag back up. She cleaned it after conducting the necropsy and later returned it to the Marines who had brought the dog to them.

A single thought ran through Vidal's mind: *Welcome to war.*

Early the next day, one of the Marines from Wrinkle's unit was waiting for the vet team. He was grief-stricken. Wrinkle had been his best friend, and he'd come to make sure that Tosca's remains made it out of Afghanistan on the same flight as Wrinkle's body.

Vidal took him down to the incinerator, but when they got there they were told the machinery needed cleaning and that it would be 24 hours before they could manage another cremation. But that would be too late. The Marine pleaded with the technician, begging him to hurry along whatever it was that needed doing. He said it was for his best friend, and told him how Wrinkle had run back into the fire when he heard Tosca barking and had died trying to save his dog and partner. They belonged together, he said, and the man finally relented.

The Marine cradled Tosca in his arms and gently surrendered the dog's body into the incinerator. He sat and waited for the four hours it took for the flames to finish their work. He didn't move from his post once the entire time, so that the dog would never be left alone. Vidal found him sitting there later with Tosca's urn held tightly in his hands. He made it in time to get her on the plane with Wrinkle, and they traveled home together.

It rained the day of Wrinkle's funeral in his hometown of Dallastown, Pennsylvania. Poured, actually. Reporters said there were two coffins in the church. The handler and his dog were buried together at the Susquehanna Cemetery.

In the Jewish tradition, it is customary, when someone dies, for a living person to sit with the body, to act as guardian from the time of death until the time of burial. The book of Jewish law called the Talmud says that during these brief hours before a body is laid to rest in the ground, the soul hovers in a space between this world and whatever lies beyond. The job of these guardians, called *shomrim,* is to comfort that soul by reading psalms and prayers aloud while keeping watch over the body to prevent any kind of desecration. It is a practice that I find reassuring. It makes death and whatever comes right after seem a little less lonely, and that's likely the true service the *shomrim* provide—a consolation for the bereaved the deceased has left behind.

Vidal, Barry, and Doughty, the veterinarian team stationed at Bagram, were the ones who waited with wounded or dead dogs and comforted their handlers until the flights came to take them home from Afghanistan, no matter the hour, day or night. They acted as the *shomrim* for the souls of the departed dogs.

During the opening stint of Vidal's yearlong deployment in Afghanistan, much of what he encountered treating MWDs seemed extreme. It wasn't the deaths that came as a shock. He was used to treating sick dogs, but Tosca had been a healthy dog. As far as he could reason, she was the victim of circumstance. Her death was sudden and violent, and that was what he found so jarring. As the days of his tour turned into weeks and then months, it all started to feel routine. Seeing dogs get blown up became normal. So Vidal numbed himself to it.

Vidal hadn't known Tosca or Wrinkle, but Barry had. That night as they viewed Tosca's body, she was transfixed by the tortured corpse, the thing that no longer resembled a dog. What, she wondered, must the Marines who died in that fire look like? She couldn't drive the thought from her mind.

Barry had dealt with a lot of tough cases with the dog teams she treated during her deployment in Afghanistan. She'd seen a lot of bad, bloody things. But that night was the only night she went home, sat on her bed, and sobbed.

49

Marine Sergeant Adam Cann was the first dog handler killed in Iraq, and the first handler killed in action since the Vietnam War.

It was the first week of January 2006. A crowd bustled outside the police recruiting station in Ramadi, Iraq. Cann and his dog Bruno were on duty along with Corporal Brendan Poelaert and his dog, Flapoor. The two soldiers stood alongside the walls of the building, eyeballing the crowd in front of them, keeping a tight rein on their dogs since there were so many people milling around. They posed for a couple of pictures. Bruno reared up on his hindquarters, teeth showing, mugging for the camera while Poelaert watched from the side. But then Cann's eyes landed on someone who gave him a bad feeling. He pushed his way through the crowd to confront the man. Reports say there was a scuffle, a deafening noise, and then only darkness.

When Poelaert came to, he was on the ground. His arm pulsed in pain. The suspicious man had been a suicide bomber. One of the ball bearings from his explosives had hit Poelaert's arm, crushing the bones at the point of contact. The impact of the blast had been so powerful and had hit with such force that ball bearings had even lodged inside Poelaert's weapon.

Poelaert looked around frantically until he saw Flapoor. Somehow the dog had managed to keep upright and was staggering only a few feet away. Poelaert could tell his dog was trying to get to him, but Flapoor was in shock. His eyes were unfocused. Blood ran in a fast current, flowing from his chest.

"I got to get my dog to the vet!" Poelaert shouted. Shrapnel had pierced Flapoor's stomach and punctured a lung.

Eventually, Poelaert and his dog were carried out of the chaos and to surgery. They would recover, as would Cann's dog, Bruno, who was also wounded in the blast. Cann did not survive.

Sometime later, Flapoor came through the ISAK course at Yuma with another handler. The instructors remembered him because the dog was so petrified of explosions. One day, while the dog teams were in the training field, a sonic boom sounded, and Flapoor took off, streaking away in fear. The instructors chased after him and found him curled up in a van, shaking. Three months later, the dog died of heart failure. But Flapoor wasn't old. His heart just gave out on him. Later, when they cremated him, they found leftover shrapnel from that day in Ramadi in the ashes.

Cann was one of 58 people killed in that 2006 bombing, just three weeks shy of his twenty-fourth birthday. He wasn't even supposed to be on patrol. He had just finished a mission but when he returned to base, he saw his friends, handlers Poelaert and Sergeant Jesse Maldonaldo, working with their dogs, and he decided to go along with them. The others told him he didn't have to do the extra work, but Cann had insisted.

After he died, the men on his base in Iraq set up a memorial, an upright slab of pocked alabaster concrete that reads

"CAMP CANN" in large, rust-colored, stenciled letters. It bears his name and the date he died. Someone sketched a likeness of Cann and Bruno onto the rough surface. It has the look and feel of a tattoo, the shading and shadows of ink on hard skin. Scrawled off to the side, in quotation marks, is "This bites for you." When the United States pulled its troops out of Iraq, the Marine Corps shipped the memorial back to Camp Pendleton, Cann's home station in California. It is now the first thing people see when they drive up to the K-9 office.

50

This tradition of military handlers memorializing their fallen is both old and well kept, as is commemorating the fallen dogs among their ranks.

Marine scout dog Kaiser, an 85-pound German shepherd, was the first dog killed in action in Vietnam. Kaiser and his handler, Lance Corporal Alfredo Salazar, were leading a patrol when they were hit with artillery fire and grenades. The dog was hit, his handler was not. It's said that Kaiser returned to his handler's side, tried to lick his hand, and then died. The Marines carried his body back to camp, buried him under the shade of a tree near their tents, and renamed their base after the dog. A red sign mounted on a wooden frame was painted with large, yellow block letters:

CAMP KAISER: THIS CAMP IS NAMED IN HONOR OF KAISER A
SCOUT DOG WHO GAVE HIS LIFE FOR HIS COUNTRY ON 6 JULY
1966 WHILE LEADING A NIGHT COMBAT PATROL IN VIET NAM.

In Afghanistan at Camp Leatherneck, near the dog kennels, there's a placard with the dark outline of a handler kneeling beside his dog. The words "From a Few of the Finest" are written on it in black. Next to it, on a painted wooden cross, "K-9 MWD" is marked in black against the wood's pale yellow. Small rectangular panels bearing the names of the dead dogs hang from the arms of the cross. When the wind blows, they move, almost like wings. In front of the cross is a small wooden podium, the top of which is made of three framed photos of fallen handlers.

If a dog is killed in action, he is memorialized and eulogized by his handlers and kennel masters at their FOBs in-country or at their home stations, or at both. These ceremonies are executed with the utmost dignity and respect. The loss is the loss of a fallen comrade, nothing more and nothing less. Open displays of mourning are appropriate, accepted.

Journalist Ernie Pyle noted this culture that embraced mourning canines after spending time with one dog on the front lines of World War II. Pyle described him as a "beautiful police dog" who belonged to "the headquarters of a regiment I knew well." Sergeant, as the dog was called by the men around him, was not only much beloved but highly intelligent. The dog had learned to run for cover when a raid flew overhead, and the men in this regiment had even dug a special foxhole just for him.

Sergeant was in his foxhole when "shrapnel from an air-burst got him." The dog's injuries were beyond treatment, so the soldiers had to put him down. Six other men died in that same attack, and while Pyle's account of that day is short, it is revealing. "The outfit lost two officers, four men and a dog in that raid. It is not belittling the men who died to say that Sergeant's death shares a big place in the grief of those who were left."

Even outside the intensity of combat theater, kennels hold formal memorial services for their dogs when they die. Handlers eulogize their partners, making full mention of their service with gratitude and respect. If you walk into an MWD kennel on any base in the United States, you're sure to come across at least one wall commemorating all the dogs who at one time or another called the site home. There's a wall at the US Air Force Academy kennels in Colorado like the one that Barry, Doughty, and Vidal had in their clinic in Bagram.

51

On one of the first days that I was out at the ISAK course in Yuma, I noticed that Kitts was wearing a black metal bracelet on his right arm. When I got close enough to take a better look, I saw that it was a memorial bracelet. It had the name Sergeant Zainah Creamer on it. She was the first female handler killed in action. She died on January 12, 2011, in Kandahar Province. Kitts had been in Afghanistan with her, and they had trained together at the beginning of their deployment. The day she was hit, he and Dyngo were being helicoptered back to FOB Wilson following a mission. The pilots gave him the news. Creamer had stepped on a pressure plate. "The waist down was gone," Kitts remembered. A medevac had come, but she had lost too much blood, and by the time they had gotten her to Kandahar, it had been too late. Her dog Jofa had not been hurt. Kitts wore the bracelet always, he said, removing it only when he showered.

Determining the number of MWD losses—precisely how many handlers and how many dogs have been killed during combat operations since the first dog teams were sent into Iraq in 2004—proved to be an unexpectedly difficult task. More difficult still is trying to calculate the number of wounded.

A few factors conspire to muddle what, from the outside, should seem easy numbers to tally. The first: There is no *centralized* official record of handlers killed in action. In fact, there never has been. There also is no official record devoted specifically to tracking combat-related injuries or deaths for dogs.

Through a variety of contacts, websites not sanctioned by the military, and news articles, I managed to pull together a number I believe is close to what an official number might look like. I started in 2004, the year that dogs first went into combat theater.

- Handlers KIA (killed in action) from 2004 to 2013: 30
- MWDs KIA from 2004 to present: 20 (2 missing in action)

That's not to say that there are not records of military handlers or their dogs, or that these teams are not kept track of while they are on deployment—or that their deaths are not noted. They certainly are. But, across all the different branches, there are many different kinds of *required* records kept, and each branch follows its own system. Of the more standard and significant type are the dogs' training and medical records, which span their military careers, but this information has many filters, and there is no point through which they intersect, save one.

There are centrally located, official, and, now, thanks to the Freedom of Information Act, publicly accessible records pertaining to MWDs. The records database is maintained by the 341st Training Squadron at Lackland Air Force Base. The Air Force, being the executive agent of the DOD's working dog program, tracks all MWDs from all branches, not just Air Force dogs. As Master Sergeant (Ret.) Joel Burton, who used to be responsible for maintaining the annually updated records, put it, this is the single document that keeps track of all DOD MWDs "from cradle to grave."

These efforts were initiated on September 27, 2000, as part of a then-new piece of legislation known as Robby's Law. This amendment was designed with a single, specific purpose, namely, "to facilitate the adoption of retired military working dogs by law enforcement agencies, former handlers of these dogs, and other persons capable of caring for these dogs." The law also mandated that the 341st Training Squadron must provide Congress a full and complete record of every dog whose military service had ended that calendar year, whether by retirement and adoption, euthanasia, or death.

But this mandate wasn't conceived in a time of war and had, and continues to have, nothing to do with the dog teams' experiences in combat. The data almost exclusively contains information pulled from veterinarians' records for each dog. Unfortunately, not all veterinarians follow the same standards or requirements. And there is no *requirement* for the notation of death to include details on how the dog was killed—whether by bullet, IED, heat exhaustion—or even a requirement to list a dog's death as killed in action.

Given that the collection of the data and its maintenance were mandated before the United States was engaged in Iraq or Afghanistan, it was simply not designed to track dogs in combat zones or what happens to them once they're there.

This all means that any record specifically devoted to the number of dogs and handlers killed in action is *not* official.

Over the years, individuals within the MWD program, some of them program managers or others in administrative roles within the 341st, have attempted to keep tabs on the teams and the losses they suffer. Even then, these records have been maintained in haphazard ways, taken on as personal rather than mandated projects.

When Lulofs and Aaslan landed in Iraq in 2004 and started to go out on missions, no one from command knew where they, or the other Air Force and Marine dog teams, were or what had happened to them. All they knew was that the teams had deployed to Iraq and were assigned to bases from there. When they were in Fallujah, Lulofs and Aaslan just went to work every day and did their job. When Lulofs finally did reach out to the Air Force Central Command, they were surprised and happy to hear from him. One guy said to Lulofs, "We were wondering where you guys were and if you were still alive."

That feeling of neglect stayed with Lulofs as he moved away from handling dogs and eventually was promoted to a job within the DOD's MWD program. There he and a few colleagues were in a position to start their own handler and dog database.

52

The inattention to where handlers went and what fates they met once they reached their deployment destination has persisted. The lack of oversight was originally a result of a simple lack of need. Until Cann's death in 2006, there was nothing in place to keep track of handlers killed in action, because no casualties or fatalities had occurred yet.

Personnel management tracking for dog handlers while they are deployed in a combat zone is an area that, Lulofs believes, has failed miserably. He is disgusted by the administrative negligence. But, for him, it's more than that. Keeping some kind of watch over deployed handlers is personal.

After Lulofs and his dog-handler partner and friend Joshua Farnsworth got back from their tour in Iraq, neither man received any medals for their service during deployment: no Purple Heart, no Bronze Star, no combat action medals or ribbons. Then Farnsworth died in July 2007.

"I never got him his medals and I promised him I would," Lulofs told me. "So I said, 'Somebody's got to keep track of these handlers.' They don't get all the help they need."

Still, the number of handlers and dogs in the MWD program together represents only a minute portion of the military's forces, and no one is, or was, thinking that keeping track of the injured or killed dogs might somehow impact the future.

This absence of practical record keeping isn't unusual in the military. As yet there isn't a standardized medical database that lists the casualties or fatalities of Iraq and Afghanistan. But during a 2010–2011 deployment in Afghanistan, Colonel Michael D. Wirt, a brigade surgeon with the 101st Airborne Division, created a unique, multilayered database that tracked wounded soldiers with remarkable detail. In this database, Wirt included criteria like "increased or decreased risk factors—whether the victim was wearing larger or smaller body armor, whether a bomb-sniffing dog was present, when a tourniquet was applied" when he listed casualties and deaths during war. He also "mapped where on the human body bullets most often struck."

Wirt's work was unique in that the information he added to basic medical record keeping was not only meticulous but also incredibly detailed. His database was intended to build a narrative and potentially to solve problems.

But for the US military, or even for each individual branch, to keep such meticulous track of all deployed servicemen and women would take an incredible amount of manpower and hours. The MWD program, at minimum, would require an across-the-board change in the way records are maintained and shared up and down the chain of command, from the veterinarians, to the handlers, to the kennel masters, to the program managers.

By the time he was deputy commander at Blanchfield Army Community Hospital, Wirt told the *New York Times* in 2012, "If you don't take data and analyze it and try to find ways to improve, then what are you doing? . . . A consolidated database with standardized input consisting of mechanism of injury and resulting wounds, classified by battle and nonbattle injuries, would be something you could actually use."

Were the MWD program to maintain a database like this, it would be setting a kind of military precedent. But its potential value for soon-to-be deploying handlers, at training facilities like ISAK at the Yuma Proving Ground, could be quite high. Knowing the details of how handlers are getting wounded or killed would be exceptionally useful. Knowing, for example, the type of IED, its size, where it was buried, how deep, and how many of them there were would also be useful. But the information, if available, is not shared, and the few people who are trying to correct the problem believe it may be impossible to shake up the system enough to inspire real change or true transparency.

Even so, there are worthy lessons to be learned.

When he was still at Yuma, Ashley had never seemed what you might call breakable. Standing well over six feet, he was, in a word, enormous. His back and shoulders were impossibly wide, earning him nicknames like Lou Ferrigno (a professional body-builder who was perhaps best known for playing The Hulk). The guys in class had all gravitated to him, all laughed at his jokes. He possessed the sure-headedness of a young man accustomed to excelling because he was big and strong.

One afternoon Ashley had coaxed Sirius up into the driver's seat of one of ISAK's golf carts and placed the dog's paws on the steering wheel. He joked with the other handlers as he made it look like Sirius was driving. If at times Ashley seemed aloof, even arrogant, with his dog he'd been gentle, working his large hands and holding his partner and pal Sirius with real delicacy, care, and respect.

part five

more dogs on duty

Usually [dogs] are quick to discover that I cannot see or hear. Truly, as companions, friends, equals in opportunities of self-expression, they unfold to me the dignity of creation.

—Helen Keller

53

The role of military working dogs in Iraq and Afghanistan has been almost exclusively devoted to combating IEDs. How much damage an IED does depends on a variety of elements, including where it is placed, how deep into the ground it's buried, how many pounds of explosives are used, and if the IED is freshly made or if it has been sitting for days or weeks. In general, it's believed that in order for someone to altogether escape the blast of an IED alive, they must be at a distance of at least 50 yards. To avoid injury from the resulting shrapnel spray, the safe distance is estimated to be about half a mile.

On May 25, 2005, the US military launched a new tactical campaign to reduce the number of deaths and injuries caused by IEDs. Called 5-and-25, it was adapted from the model British forces had used with success in Northern Ireland. The idea was that when a convoy or patrol stops and dismounts from their vehicles, the first thing a unit does is clear a distance of about 5 yards around the vehicle, spanning out until a perimeter of about 25 yards is cleared. In the three weeks before the Army officially pushed out the 5-and-25 program, no fewer than 52 US service members were killed in Iraq, many of them by IEDs.

As the rate of IEDs continued to increase, so did the Pentagon's efforts to counter them. In 2006, the DOD created the Joint Improvised Explosive Device Defeat Organization (JIEDDO). Its sole purpose, and its many billions of dollars in funding, was to combat IEDs. Over the next few years, JIEDDO spent upward of $19 billion pursuing numerous technological innovations, from handler sensors to aerial sensors to enhanced optics.

In 2010 JIEDDO's director, Lieutenant General Michael Oates, gave a report on the organization's progress. After all the money spent and all the tools developed during those years, Oates said the best detection ability US forces had against the threat of IEDs was a handler and his detection dog.

Nearly two years later, in September 2012, the man who succeeded Oates as head of JIEDDO, Lieutenant General Michael D. Barbero, addressed the Subcommittee of Defense of the US House of Representatives Committee on Appropriations in Washington, DC. Barbero reported that the threat would not only persist but would become even more deadly in the future. US forces were going to continue to operate in an IED environment. That was, Barbero testified, a reality of twenty-first-century warfare, and the country must prepare accordingly.

The IED had surpassed artillery as being the greatest killer on the modern battlefield. "The IED and the networks that employ these asymmetric weapons," Barbero said, "are here to stay—operationally and here at home."

So while the United States may have removed its forces from Iraq and is drawing down its troops in Afghanistan, the rate of IED use is expected to climb in the coming months and years—and not just in these battleground countries. Modern warfare's deadliest weapon is not only here to stay, but there's reason to think that the United States is not and will not be immune. In the past 20 years, the United States has endured three massively destructive incidents in which explosives were used to incite terror and cause mass casualties—in Waco, Texas, in

1993; in the Oklahoma City, Oklahoma, bombing, in 1995; and in the Boston Marathon bombing in Massachusetts, in 2013.

In truth, the battleground of bombs on American soil began many years before Waco. And when it did, there were actually dogs trained to find them and protect our homeland, even if few people knew about them.

54

At 11:30 on the morning of Tuesday, March 7, 1972, an anonymous caller phoned the headquarters of Trans World Airlines (TWA). The voice on the line alerted TWA to a 25-cent rental locker in Kennedy International Airport's TWA terminal. The New York officials who searched the locker found two large Army duffel bags and a note demanding ransom in the amount of $2 million. If it was not paid, the note said, bombs planted on four of the airline's flights would detonate at six-hour intervals. TWA security was notified, and so began a 24-hour race against the clock that sent panic to the skies and to airports all over the world. The airline had thousands of passengers scheduled to fly in approximately 240 planes, and the task of finding the bombs in time seemed nearly impossible.

By the time officials determined the threat was indeed legitimate and put out a call to all TWA flights for an immediate and mandatory bomb search, a host of planes were already airborne. One of these flights, a West Coast–bound Boeing 707, was already more than 100 miles into its nonstop flight to Los Angeles. It had been in the air only 15 minutes when the pilot, Captain William Motz, came over the intercom to tell the 45 passengers and the seven-person crew that they were headed back to New York, citing mechanical difficulties.

Motz landed the plane and taxied to a remote part of the runway, a good distance from the main hub of the airport. It was ten minutes past noon. If there was a bomb on the plane, it was set to go off at 1 p.m. The passengers were hurried off the aircraft. The police, who were already waiting on the tarmac, rushed aboard. With them were two search dogs. Brandy, a German shepherd, and her handler, David Connally, worked the front end of the plane. Another police officer worked toward the back with Sally, a Labrador. Inside the cockpit, Brandy was nosing her way around a large black case marked "Crew." It was a nondescript piece of pilot gear, the kind of case that carried a flight manual. But after a few good sniffs, Brandy sank her haunches into a resolved sit. Connally knew they'd found the bomb, and he signaled the others. The time was 12:48 p.m.

Detective William F. Schmitt of the police department's bomb squad called for all the officers to get off the plane. He cut into the case and quickly scanned its contents. He saw what he guessed to be roughly six pounds of plastic C-4 explosives with a fuse rigged to a timer. It was enough, he knew, to rip the plane to shreds. In a fast decision, Schmitt picked up that clunky, ticking case and carried it off the plane and onto the runway, moving quickly away from the crowd of people. After setting down the case on the ground, Schmitt disabled the bomb. The time was 12:55 p.m.

The very next day, a bomb hidden inside another TWA plane in Las Vegas exploded. The plane, which had been sitting idle and empty at the time, had been searched, but the bomb was in the cockpit and had gone undiscovered. No one was injured, but a panic ensued. By noon that day, two of the airline's pilots refused to fly, and TWA's business was down 50 percent.

In response to the bombs and the public concern, a Federal Aviation Adminstration representative, Lieutenant General (Ret.) Benjamin Davis, sat in front of TV cameras and in a grave tone warned that his organization was now engaged in a "war for the survival of the air transportation industry." By the end of that week, President Richard Nixon gave orders to Transportation Secretary John A. Volpe to push into action early security measures that were already in development as part of the response to recent hijacking attempts made on American flights. Travelers would now be subjected to mandatory passenger and baggage screenings. Airline and cargo facilities would now be off limits to unauthorized personnel. Nixon also ordered the secretary of transportation to create a force that included dogs. That same year, the Federal Aviation Administration started its Detection Canine Team Program.

55

The dog program that was born out of Brandy's heroic find in 1972 evolved under different agencies, and after 9/11, the canine program was transferred to the Transport Security Administration (TSA), which would become part of the Department of Homeland Security the following year. There are now over 900 canine teams working in 120 airports nationwide.

The two bomb dog teams that patrolled the terminal in the Colorado Springs airport when I visited in December 2011 were an outgrowth of that original program's creation. Colorado State police officer Mike Anderson and his dog, Cezar, and fellow officer Wayne Strader and his dog, Rex, are part of the TSA Bomb Dog Program that began at this airport in 2005.

There was something about being followed by a big German shepherd and a police officer in uniform that made my heart skip and my legs twitch with the urge to run. I was pulling a smooth-gliding and nondescript black carry-on suitcase, possibly the most ordinary piece of luggage on the planet. And it was empty, except for the explosives packed inside. I was trying to act as normal as possible because I didn't want anything other than the odor of the explosive material to tip off the dog.

I kept walking straight as I felt the dog team about to pass me. The dog had already picked up the scent. His body swiveled with intense interest, and that alone was enough to signal to his handler that there was something in my bag. The dog made this find, as well as a series of others that day throughout the airport, without trouble. Anderson was especially happy with Cezar's performance, because the dog was getting older and Anderson had noticed that he had started to slow down.

Unlike military working dogs, TSA bomb-sniffing dogs live with their handlers, and their careers together can span the dogs' working lives. Both of these teams had been partnered together for more than six years. That is why Anderson was sad that Cezar wasn't performing like he used to. It meant that their work together would soon be coming to an end.

On the day I was there, the terminal at the Colorado Springs airport wasn't very crowded, and the few passengers sitting and waiting for their flights to board took great interest in the dogs. Some people pointed and smiled curiously, while a few eyed large Cezar warily. That visibility, Officer Strader explained, is a big part of the role they play in keeping the airport secure. Cezar and Rex do their jobs simply by being on the job, acting as a visual deterrent and causing any would-be criminal to think twice. Most of the time, Rex and Cezar search unattended bags or vehicles left without a driver by the curb. In addition to their post at the airport, they also respond to any bomb threats in the city.

Despite the increased K-9 security presence in airports, most airports rely almost entirely on scanning machines to check luggage and passengers. Airport security depends heavily on a series of electronic scanners and full-body imaging machines that have stirred up controversy. There are concerns not only that the machines invade personal privacy but that they are also ineffective.

During a July 2011 congressional hearing, House of Representatives members listened to testimony from TSA representatives; the former director of security at Ben Gurion International Airport in Tel Aviv, Israel; and an inspector with the Amtrak Police Department's K-9 unit, among others, in order to evaluate the current state of US airport security and Department of Homeland Security policies. Congressman Jason Chaffetz, a Republican from Utah, led the inquiry and did not mince words as he kicked off his opening remarks, citing a long list of concerns. Chief among them: Since November 2001, there had been 25,000 security breaches at US airports.

From there the hearing unfolded in high drama, especially when explosive-detection dogs were brought into the discussion. Proponents of canine detection teams went head to head with those advocating machines. Among the many issues that were hotly debated were invasion of privacy, the longevity of million-dollar machines that proved ineffectual, and the cost of Alpo dog food.

During the height of this inquiry and testimony, Chaffetz brought up the Pentagon's conclusion that dogs were the best bomb detectors. He then leveled a challenge at TSA assistant administrator John Sammon:

> You're suggesting that the whole body imaging machine is a cheaper alternative than using the K-9s. I tell you what, let's do this. I would love to do this. I would love to do this. You take 1,000 people and put them in a room, I will give you 10 whole body imagining [sic] machines. You give me 5,000 people in another room and you give me one of [the] dogs, and we will find the bomb before you find your bomb.
>
> That is the problem. There is a better, smarter, safer way to do this. And the TSA is not prioritizing it. And if you look at who those lobbyists were that pushed through those machines, they should be ashamed of themselves, because there is a better way to do this and it is with the K-9s.

56

They made it into Baghdad on Monday night, May 11, 2009. It was already very late by the time Army Captain Cecilia Najera's flight from Tikrit landed. Najera was uneasy about this trip, but when she looked down she was contented. Her partner, a black Labrador retriever named Boe, whom she called her "little shadow," was close beside her.

Lieutenant Colonel Beth Salisbury, commander of the Camp Liberty Stress Clinic, was there to pick them up. Najera and Boe climbed into her vehicle. Salisbury looked and sounded exhausted as she briefed Najera on what they would be walking into that night.

Earlier that day, Army Sergeant John M. Russell, a patient, had walked into the clinic and opened fire on fellow servicemen, patients, and staff, killing five people and wounding three others. Russell, who was on his third deployment, had been escorted to the clinic that morning, not by his own choosing but on his commander's insistence. Russell had been exhibiting alarming behavior and was openly expressing thoughts of suicide. In fact, he had already been to the clinic on four separate occasions, and, only three days earlier, his commander had disabled Russell's weapon by removing the bolt so that it couldn't be fired. But when Russell got to the clinic, he became belligerent and was told to leave.

Just one hour later, he fought with the soldier placed as his escort and took his weapon, an M16 rifle. He then forced the man from the car at gunpoint and returned to the stress clinic. The soldier alerted military police, but by the time they tried to warn the clinic's staff, it was too late. The military police on the phone with the clinic said they could hear shots being fired on the other end of the phone line.

Najera and Boe hadn't been sent to Iraq to find IEDs or drugs or to work patrols. This dog team was there as part of a new Army initiative. Najera had deployed to Iraq with the 528th Medical Detachment Combat and Operational Stress Control (COSC) Unit. Boe, her partner, was a combat-trained therapy dog.

It was pure coincidence that Najera and Boe had arrived in Baghdad on the same day. Najera and Boe had visited Camp Liberty's clinic before, and they knew the people who had been inside during the attack. Which was part of why Najera was uneasy, scared even. Not only was she unsure of what she and Boe were about to encounter, but she was at a loss to think of what she could do to be of any real help. The people in this clinic weren't just soldiers, they were also therapists and doctors, health-care professionals just like she was. What could she possibly say, she wondered, that would make a difference to any of them?

"I'm not sure that they're going to want to talk to you," Salisbury warned her as they drove, as if reading Najera's mind. The clinic, she said, had been inundated with offers of support, but she doubted any outsider would be able or even welcome to do much for her staff. Not tonight at least, she said. It was too soon.

The military police had sealed off the clinic as a crime scene, so the staff was in the small adjacent building that housed the commander's office. Najera and Boe waited in the hallway with the others who had come to lend their services. There were chaplains, a social worker, and other mental health-care providers. They all stood in silence until a sergeant emerged from the room where the clinic staff had gathered together. She addressed the group in the hall. "No one on staff wants to see anyone," she said, and told them all to leave. Najera turned to shuffle out with the others, but then she heard the sergeant's voice again. "Ma'am?" The woman was addressing Najera. "You and Boe can come in."

Inside, the clinic staff sat without speaking. Their eyes were red and raw, whether from crying or exhaustion, Najera couldn't tell. She simply nodded at the group, slipped into a chair, and unclipped Boe's leash, so the dog could have the run of the room. Boe wove her way in and around the chairs, sniffing and greeting people as she encountered them. The sergeant who had invited them to stay called Boe over and kept the dog next to her, patting her large black head.

Once or twice someone broke the silence. One of the younger staffers, a woman, wanted to talk about what had hap-

pened. But after she spoke, the group went mute again. It had
been a long day for Najera and for Boe. The dog was tired,
and they hadn't planned on working straight from the plane,
so Najera hadn't dressed Boe in her vest, which was a signal to
the dog that she was in work mode. So, being tired herself, Boe
plopped down in the middle of the room with little grace and
released a heavy, grunting sigh.

A few people chuckled at this. Some small smiles showed,
even if briefly. And Najera felt reassured. The dog had just done
what probably every person there had wanted to do, and though
it was a mild kind of relief, for the smallest of moments the tension broke and the room lightened.

57

Between 2007 and 2011, eight dogs made up the very first
COSC dog therapy teams: Boe, Budge, Zeke, Albert,
Butch, Zach, Apollo, and Timmy. They were the first therapy
dogs ever trained and deployed to combat theaters in Iraq and
Afghanistan.

The idea to deploy COSC dogs hatched in 2007, after those working with wounded soldiers at the Walter Reed
Army Medical Center in Washington, DC, began to notice
that service dogs, assigned to help wounded soldiers get used
to prosthetic limbs, were as integral to each patient's emotional
recovery as to their physical recovery. Cases of animal-assisted
therapy for people recovering from severe injuries or trauma
were well documented. So why did soldiers have to wait until
they were wounded to benefit? Why, these therapists wondered,

couldn't this kind of restorative interaction be applied preemptively in a combat theater?

The Army partnered with America's VetDogs (a nonprofit organization started by the Guide Dog Foundation for the Blind) and developed a program that would bring skilled therapy dogs into the combat theater.

The idea was simple. The dogs would become part of the combat stress control units, attached to occupational therapists who would also receive additional training to become therapy-dog handlers. The COSC units were mobile, meaning that they traveled from FOBs to patrol bases. They essentially acted as a door-to-door resource, bringing stress and trauma relief to servicemen and women in the combat zone. The dogs were intended to serve as icebreakers for deployed service members. They were a way to make it easier for servicepeople to begin to speak to the human therapists.

COSC dogs required much of the same pre-deployment preparedness training as MWDs. The dogs had to be exposed to the different kinds of terrain they would encounter. They also needed to become used to the feel of earmuffs and goggles and the sounds of live gunfire, explosions, large military aircraft, and helicopters. Unlike MWDs, COSC dogs had to be adaptable to multiple handlers and fill different roles. Their disposition was of the utmost importance. These dogs had to have close to the perfect temperament to be effective.

In December 2007, the first two COSC dogs deployed to Iraq. They were a pair of matching black Labs: Special First Class Budge and Special First Class Boe.

Boe was a quiet dog, lumbering and sweet, with a molasses-mellow temperament. As an occupational therapist who had volunteered to be a COSC dog handler, Najera saw the difference Boe made with her patients almost instantly. Boe wasn't popular just with the soldiers but with command as well. While Najera had anticipated resistance to the idea of therapy in the theater of war, she found that with Boe, her presence was not just accepted, but welcomed with enthusiasm.

Still, Najera trod lightly. She never forced Boe on anyone. The dog, however, was gentle enough that Najera often could let her roam off the leash. Boe had a knack for seeking out reluctant and withdrawn soldiers who might be too shy or traumatized to ask for help from another soldier.

Boe did not just help soldiers who were deeply affected. She also helped others with more mundane problems. At one point during their tour, Najera noticed that Boe had gained quite a bit of weight from all the treats she had been given. Najera realized that a soldier who liked to visit Boe had also been gaining weight. It was slowing him down, and he was having a hard time finding the energy to motivate himself to exercise. So Najera used Boe as a way to engage him and never really directly addressed his weight issue. Instead, she made it about Boe's weight. Pretty soon, the soldier was taking the dog out on runs a few times a week. He had decided they would lose weight together.

Boe was effective in even more subtle ways. Najera began to see soldiers put their hands on the dog without any prompting and then, finally, begin to open up about their problems. Others simply liked being around the dog, approaching Boe because they just wanted to hug her before they continued about their day.

When they started their duties in Tikrit, Najera and Boe made regular visits to the combat support hospital. It was a US military facility, but the staff there treated Iraqi civilians as well.

Captain Cecilia Najera poses with her COSC dog, Boe, in 2009 in Iraq, where they served together for 15 months.

Credit: Rebecca Frankel

They treated anyone who was injured as a result of the war, even insurgents. While in the hospital, Najera was always careful not to approach Iraqi patients with Boe, as she was aware that there were cultural differences between the way many Americans and many Iraqis regarded dogs. In Iraq, dogs are generally considered unclean, and they are not kept as pets.

In urban areas of Iraq, dogs run wild in the streets. The stray dog population reached epic proportions in 2010. After a series of attacks on residents of Baghdad, the Iraqi government took action and deployed some 20 teams of veterinarians and police to shoot or poison the dogs. They killed upward of 58,000 stray dogs in three months.

However, Najera and Boe made so many trips to the hospital together that the civilian patients and their visiting families grew familiar with the dog team. They sometimes smiled or laughed when Boe passed by.

One patient was an Iraqi girl around 12 years old. According to the story Najera was told, the girl's parents were both insurgents who had been killed during a raid by US forces. The girl was shot after she herself apparently reached for a weapon. A bullet hit her in the abdomen and went into her small intestines. It wreaked havoc on her insides and then exited her colon. She had a colostomy bag and had been confined to bed for many months. The girl was so frail and small that she appeared years younger than she actually was.

Each time Boe passed by, the girl watched with large dark eyes. Najera assumed the girl was afraid of the dog. So, when one of the nurses approached her and said that she thought the girl would really like it if Boe visited her bedside, Najera was surprised and somewhat reluctant. The nurse insisted. The staff had been giving their patient Play-Doh to occupy the long stretches of bed confinement. Each time the girl fashioned the clay into small, brightly colored dogs.

For Boe's first visits to the girl, Najera took it slowly. She kept the dog at a distance. The girl would smile. Then Najera would do tricks with Boe, like "sit," "shake," and "lie down," and the girl would laugh. It took a few weeks, but finally the girl reached out a cautious hand and touched the dog. As she recovered over the six months of her hospital stay, the girl was eventually able to get up from bed. Not long after that, she took to walking Boe up and down the hallways. When she was with Boe, the girl seemed genuinely happy.

The night of the shooting at Camp Liberty's clinic, the forecast called for a huge sandstorm. That and other transportation delays kept Najera and Boe there for a week. Initially Najera was frustrated that she and Boe were unable to find a flight back to Tikrit, but later she felt grateful. There were five memorial services held that week for the clinic staff, and she and Boe attended each one.

That was when the tears came. Those were some very long and challenging days for the COSC dog team. There were no breaks. Najera and Boe worked straight through the day and into the night. It was the hardest week of their 15-month deployment. But Najera felt that she and Boe were meant to be there to help in the aftermath of such a tragic event. That's why she and Boe were in Iraq.

58

No one is entirely sure why Russell snapped that day, or what drove him to kill five people. According to a 325-page report published in October 2009 investigating the incident, he'd been exhibiting erratic behavior for weeks and threatening suicide. When this mental break occurred, Russell had been just six weeks from finishing his third deployment to Iraq. While his rampage was unprecedentedly deadly, he was far from the first soldier to crack under the strain of combat.

Since the Iraq and Afghanistan wars, posttraumatic stress disorder (PTSD) has been so prevalent among US servicemen and women that it has earned classification as an outright epidemic. Of the soldiers, Marines, airmen, and sailors who come home from Iraq and Afghanistan, one in five has PTSD, adding up to 300,000 so far.

Untreated and unaddressed, PTSD frequently leads to volatile behavior and suicide. The rate of suicide among active-duty service members, as well as among recent veterans, is alarming. Currently, every 80 minutes a veteran takes his own life. From 2005 to 2010, a service member committed suicide once every 36 hours. The 1 percent of Americans who have served in the US military make up 20 percent of the country's suicides. "Suicide," as journalist Tina Rosenberg reported in September 2012, "is now the leading cause of death in the Army."

Though combat stress dogs like Boe are few, canine therapy is a growing trend, one that continues to gain legitimacy in the world of psychotherapy. And dogs have long been regarded as therapeutic tools for psychologically wounded patients and for physically wounded servicemen as well.

During World War I, military dogs deployed by the French Legion who were no longer able to fulfill their combat duties were retrained to be companions of blind soldiers. They were taught to anticipate approaching cars, alert their charge to drops and inclines in the road, and guide the soldier safely to the homes of friends and family. The process for acquiring such a dog was fairly uncomplicated. Men who needed a guide dog simply sent letters to the War Dog Service. But as Harold Baynes reported from France, despite the accessibility of the dogs, it wasn't a very popular service. This, he wrote, was largely "because of the feeling that a blind man led by a dog must necessarily appear to be an object of charity." Disappointingly, this assessment was representative of the time.

Then the November 5, 1927, edition of the *Saturday Evening Post* featured a stirring article by a woman named Dorothy Harrison Eustis. Eustis had just traveled to Potsdam, Germany, where she saw firsthand how Germany was rehabilitating its "war blind." What she witnessed had a profound effect on her and would forever change her thinking about the future of any blind person:

> *In darkness and uncertainty he must start again, wholly dependent on outside help for every move. His other senses may rally to his aid, but they cannot replace his eyesight. To man's never failing friend has been accorded this special privilege. Gentlemen, I give you the German shepherd dog. . . .*
>
> *No longer dependent on a member of the family, a friend or a paid attendant, the blind can once more take up their normal lives as nearly as possible where they left them off.*

In a small Tennessee town, a man read Eustis's article out loud to his blind son, Morris Frank. The young man had lost his right eye in a riding accident when he was six years old. The left eye was damaged beyond repair 10 years later during a high school boxing match. The young Frank was so inspired by Eustis's experience that he sent her a letter four days later, asking her for the address of the German school for the blind and service dogs. She responded saying she would take Frank abroad to receive his education at the school for the blind. In return, she wanted him to promise to show off his success and promote the cause once he returned to the States.

Frank agreed and traveled overseas, where he was paired with a dog named Kiss, whom he quickly renamed Buddy. By the time their training was completed, Frank was moving around with Buddy with total comfort and ease. When the pair made the trip back home and docked in New York, a crowd of spectators had gathered, including reporters who had come armed with photographers. It was a skeptical if not altogether unkind crowd, and one reporter shouted out, daring Frank to cross West Street to prove to them all what a dog could do for a blind man.

West Street was a high-speed interstate of danger compared to where Frank had been overseas. Buddy had never ventured out in anything like this. Cabbies jeered out car windows, trucks barreled past them, horns honked from all sides. Frank lifted his foot off the curb. For the next three long minutes he relinquished all control to his dog. To the shock of all watching, they made it across without a hitch. Frank dropped his arms around Buddy, jubilant and relieved, his heart still thudding. "Good girl, good girl," he commended her.

Eight years later, Frank and Buddy had put in 50,000 miles preaching the good word of guide dogs. They forever changed the perception of guide dogs for the blind. They helped to establish the Seeing Eye School in Morristown, New Jersey, in 1929. By 1936, the school had paired dogs with 250 blind men and women.

When Japan bombed Pearl Harbor and the United States entered World War II, Eustis and Frank, still friends and colleagues, rejoined forces to make sure that war veterans who needed guide dogs received them.

59

As early as 1919, the US military brought dogs in as therapy tools for World War I psychiatric patients at St. Elizabeth's Hospital in Washington, DC. But it was during World War II that dogs really made their mark helping veterans recover from war.

The Associated Press filed a report direct from the Anzio beachhead in Italy of a dog named Lulabelle. Lieutenant Colonel William E. King, a chaplain, was making his rounds of a hospital tent visiting the beds of the wounded. On this particular day, he'd brought along his dog, Lulabelle, who was so small she often made these visits in the chaplain's pocket. One of the nurses stopped the chaplain and pointed out a soldier who was lying on his back and had his gaze fixed on the ceiling. He had lost both hands and was, the nurse said, lucky to be alive. He'd been virtually nonresponsive since they brought him to the hospital. But when he saw Lulabelle, he tried to speak. The chaplain went over to his bed to see what he wanted. The man asked the chaplain to put the dog on his bed. Lulabelle obligingly scrambled across the man's chest to lick his face.

"I used to have a dog, sir," the man explained. "That's the first time a dog has licked my face since I left home." And then he smiled. When the chaplain left the hospital that day, he did so without Lulabelle. Instead she stayed on that bed, curled up with the young man, her head resting over his shoulder.

In the summer of 1944, a similar encounter and act of benevolence would bring canines into the halls of the American Air Forces Convalescent Hospital in Pawling, New York. A Red Cross volunteer got the idea that a dog might break the melancholy of one recuperating airman, a Lieutenant Colin, who had a shattered leg. Dogs for Defense, the very same organization responsible for providing the US military with its first-ever official canine fighting force, arranged for Colin to get a German shepherd puppy named Fritz. The change in Colin was extraordinary. He improved so much that his recovery time exceeded his doctors' expectations by six months.

Fritz's presence and Colin's undeniable progress kicked off a small movement at the hospital. Soon other patients were asking for their own dogs.

And, just as they had during World War I, war dogs who had been wounded or had finished their tour of service were paired with wounded soldiers to become healing companions. Soon hospitals in Massachusetts and in New York State were requesting and receiving dogs for their patients. Nearly two years after Lieutenant Colin was paired with Fritz, the hospital in Pawling installed an 80-foot kennel fully outfitted to house 50 dogs.

As one former pilot and a convalescent hospital patient who benefited from this movement wrote, "The Red Cross got me Patty, the swellest Irish Setter you ever saw. We're never apart. . . . And I've been feeling better since the day I got her."

Over the next few decades, animal-assisted therapy slowly began attracting attention in the civilian world. Therapist Boris Levinson, owner of a dog named Jingles, once forgot to remove the dog from the room during a therapy session, only to notice that a young patient, a withdrawn boy, became noticeably more relaxed with Jingles there. Levinson took note of this canine-inspired improvement, and Jingles became a regular fixture in his therapy sessions. In 1962, Levinson published an article on the phenomenon, "The Dog as Co-Therapist."

It would take until the 1990s for there to be strong scientific evidence that dogs have a tremendously positive effect on lowering stress and anxiety. A 1998 study showed that, after a half hour spent with a dog, psychiatric patients exhibited a reduction in their anxiety that was two times that of other, more standard stress-alleviating therapeutic activities. In 2003, the woman who conducted this study, Sandra Barker of Virginia Commonwealth University, reported that patients awaiting electroconvulsive therapy were less fearful after spending 15 minutes with a dog. The American Heart Association released a study in 2005 that showed that 12 minutes of time spent with therapy dogs improved "heart and liver function, reduced blood pressure, diminished harmful hormones, and decreased anxiety in heart patients."

So convincing was this and other data that in 2009, Senator Al Franken, a Democrat from Minnesota, and Senator Johnny Isakson, a Republican from Georgia, drafted and passed the Service Dogs for Veterans Act. The bill mandated that no fewer than 200 service dogs would be paired with US veterans and that these dogs should be divided evenly between those suffering from physical injuries and those suffering "primarily from mental health difficulties." In tandem with this pilot program were plans for a three-year scientific study of the initiative within the Department of Veterans Affairs to determine the therapeutic benefits to veterans, from quality of life to savings on health-care costs. And the following year, the federal government committed to spending several million dollars to gather scientific evidence on the impact that dogs have on PTSD.

But it wasn't the research that inspired the arrival of the first therapy dog at Walter Reed National Military Medical Center in 2007. It was an accidental observation very much like the one made at Pawling during World War II. At the height of the Iraq War, occupational therapist Harvey Naranjo, a former combat medic, was watching his patients while they were at the stables for equine therapy. Riding horses helped work the patients' core muscles. A few dogs were also ambling around the barn. Naranjo saw his most withdrawn patient playing with one of the dogs, The man looked so much happier and more relaxed. Naranjo commented offhandedly to a man standing nearby that having a dog at Walter Reed would make his job a lot easier. The man turned out to be a retired Army veterinary officer who took Naranjo's idea seriously. Within a short time, they had their first trained service dog on staff, a chocolate Lab named Deuce.

The positive impact that Deuce had on everyone he encountered at Walter Reed was what inspired the Warrior Transition Brigade's Wounded Warrior Service Dog Training Program in 2009. The program was designed to use dogs to prepare recovering patients for the life transition they would make once they left the hospital, whether it was to return to military service, go back to school, or find employment in the civilian world.

There were two ideas behind the program. In addition to spending time with the dogs, the recovering soldiers would be training them to be service dogs for veterans. The program worked miraculously well. Patients previously unable to perform everyday tasks were suddenly empowered and able to accomplish them once they were next to a young puppy.

While the program wasn't limited to soldiers struggling with PTSD, they were often the best candidates. The dogs not only provided soldiers who had been withdrawn or depressed with calming and unconditionally loving company, but their presence also gave them the motivation to get out of bed and provided them with a prideful purpose. Despite the fact that these soldiers knew their dogs weren't going to belong to them forever, the effect was profound.

Even the patients' families reported seeing a change. Training a young puppy takes a steady, careful hand and a willingness to emote happiness and praise. The necessary exercise of offering the dog a reward for good work requires a particular tone that combines neutrality with high-pitched and joyful enthusiasm. By interacting with the dogs in this manner, over time, patients relearned a more gentle way to interact with their spouses and children, even if only subconsciously. Their voices were transformed from the flat, dejected affect so typical of PTSD into something more upbeat and engaged.

60

Sara Hook was the chief of the Warrior Transition Brigade's Occupational Therapy Department when the dog program started at Walter Reed. She remembers one soldier in particular who came into the military hospital. He was confined to a wheelchair and had a combination of psychological and physical wounds. Like many newly admitted patients, he was closed off. He always had his head down and kept his eyes low. But when therapy dogs approached him, Hook observed an instant transformation. By the time this patient completed the program some six months later, he was able to stand at a podium and speak from a microphone in front of a crowded room and lead an official military ceremony. Of course, he had other traditional rehabilitative therapy while at Walter Reed, but Hook believes this soldier will say that it was the dogs that made the difference. They offered unconditional love and were always happy to see him, no matter how he looked or felt and regardless of his being in a wheelchair.

Hook and her staff at Walter Reed were not the only ones to see changes in their patients after the dog program began. Case managers also reported that there was a decrease in prescriptions for medications for pain, anxiety, and depression. Yet so far the evidence supporting the success of this kind of stepping-stone therapy program at Walter Reed is largely anecdotal. Scientific studies have not yet been conducted to analyze the efficacy of the dog program.

Captain Najera faced a similar problem. Even though Boe's positive impact was clear to the observant eye, Najera had difficulty building a clear case among the military's top brass for continuing the use of therapy dogs.

During her deployment, Najera started collecting data for a research paper, one that would examine what evidence, if any, would show that the therapy dogs were making a difference. She compared the dogs with three other therapeutic techniques: guided imagery (envisioning a safe, happy place), deep breathing exercises, and basic education on coping with stress. But conducting the surveys proved difficult. It was hard to assess the range of the dogs' impact. While Najera and Boe had regular visits with patients, she could not account for everyone who might have found relief in Boe's presence. And then, just as they were collecting this data, things for the US military in Iraq began to change. The drawdown of troops started, and

servicemen and women were transferred out of their bases in
Iraq. Najera and the other occupational therapist–dog handlers
lost track of the soldiers in their survey pool. One day the soldiers were there with Boe and the other dogs, then, suddenly,
they were gone.

Boe was in Iraq for a total of 18 months. She served two deployments back to back. Toward the end of their second tour,
Najera started to see a change in Boe. She had never been the
kind of dog who relished being the center of a large crowd, but
she'd always accepted the affection offered to her and indulged
the excited fuss the soldiers made with friendly patience.

But after nearly 15 months of being Boe's handler, Najera
noticed that when soldiers approached Boe, she turned away
from them. The only time she seemed happy was when she was
free to just be a dog. She didn't want to engage anymore. It was
as if, Najera says, she had absorbed too much sadness.

It would be counterintuitive, even foolhardy, to assume
that dogs can experience war but be somehow immune to its
hardships and burdens. Dogs experience the same heat, the
same chaos, the same injuries, the same violence, and the same
trauma. War and combat affect all dogs, just the way they do
soldiers. And like people, each dog responds differently. But
because working dogs are in such high demand, and their numbers are relatively few compared to their handlers, they do not
take breaks between deployments as their handlers do. Dogs
with good working records who are in good health may be
deployed more times and more often than their handlers, and
they often serve back-to-back tours. This takes a toll. Military
working dogs, like soldiers, return from war changed.

61

In March 2012, at the ISAK course in Yuma, a large German shepherd named Jessy stared down the long, sandy stretch of unpaved desert road. She was uneasy. There were bomb-sniffing aids buried about 100 yards from where she was standing, and her Army handler, Sergeant Sabrina Curtis, was trying to coax her forward. She commanded the dog to search alone, off leash.

But something held Jessy back. She moved cautiously, haltingly, casting her head back as if at any moment she expected to turn and find Curtis vanished. Curtis, a diminutive handler with a soft but firm voice, repeated her command to search, this time with more force. Jessy put her nose to the ground and set to work, eagerly moving about 10 feet ahead. She gave all the cues to indicate she was working on detecting an odor, which was promising. But then she suddenly pulled up and away from the odor to check again on Curtis. The dog looked torn, almost gloomy. After a few more hesitant steps and several nervous glances backward, it became clear that this dog was more than merely reluctant to search away from her handler.

When Jessy's previous handler went on leave, the dog just broke down. The handler's sudden departure set off a bout of separation anxiety. During his absence, Jessy would spin compulsively in her crate, so frequently that she broke her tail not once but twice. The veterinarians who treated her removed a length of it rather than have it suffer any further breaks.

Curtis and Jessy gave it a few more tries before Sergeant Charlie Hardesty, who had been observing the pair, walked out to join them. He led Jessy to the source of the odor to make the find and rewarded her with the Kong. She still looked back at Curtis, but she sat at the source and, when Hardesty praised her, she responded well. The handlers wanted to keep things positive for Jessy and to get her to associate reward and affection with working rather than with whatever was keeping her from feeling confident and secure on patrol.

To see Jessy's lack of confidence is to know that war wounds, whether skin deep or the kind that are made on the inside, can have an equally damaging and similar effect on a dog.

Canine posttraumatic stress disorder, or CPTSD, is a relatively new term that's only recently been applied in a serious and consistent way in the military veterinary field. When the number of dogs on the ground in Afghanistan and Iraq reached its height in 2011, it was reported that 5 percent of the 650 dogs deployed were developing CPTSD. The chief of behavioral medicine at Lackland's MWD hospital, Dr. Walter E. Burghardt Jr., estimated that half of those dogs would have to retire from service.

The war dogs who were at the veterinary clinic at Bagram were right in the midst of the fighting. They were constantly around popping bullets and booming explosions. Some of them had to be medevaced for CPTSD and treated with drugs, the equivalent of canine Prozac. Human PTSD is hard to treat, but CPTSD has its own set of challenges. "You can't tell a dog it's going to be okay, you can't explain to him what's going on," said Captain Katie Barry. Researching the topic is especially challenging, because you can't replicate the trauma of combat at home, nor would you want to, and as a result, research on CPTSD is still scarce and evolving.

Part of the problem might just be that some of the dogs should not have been taken into a combat situation to begin with. Not every war dog trainer is like Jakubin. He exposed the dogs at the USAF Academy kennels to different types of environmental situations that they could encounter in the field, everything from flights of stairs to large crowds and loud noises. He pushed them to test their resolve. A dog who might be a daring detection dog inside a quiet building may quickly lose his drive in an unfamiliar setting or a place he finds stressful.

During the March 2012 ISAK course, the instructors were concerned with about 3 of the 17 dogs who attended. These were dogs they felt needed more than three weeks of training to be deployment ready. It was possible that these dogs' war dog days, like Jessy's, were already behind them. It was possible that these dogs just shouldn't be responsible for the safety of others in a combat zone.

But even capable teams and dogs who show promise and courage in training, and give all the signs that they are ready to tackle a combat deployment, are susceptible to being traumatized once they're downrange.

62

US Army handler Staff Sergeant Donald Craig Miller and his Belgian Malinois, Ody, deployed to Afghanistan in late September 2012 but returned only a few months later in January 2013. What was supposed to be a yearlong deployment ended early. A great detection dog, Ody hit odor and rarely fell victim to distraction during patrols or searches on base back home. When Miller left their home station, Fort Rucker in Alabama, he felt confident in his dog, knowing they would be able to handle the elite missions they were going to be executing.

When they got to Afghanistan, they were attached to a MARSOC unit, bunking in a compound near Camp Leatherneck, the 1,600-acre Marine Corps base that is home to 10,000 troops. Their initial training together on base went well. Ody was his reliable, happy-dog self. He adjusted well to the temperature and their lodgings on base. Miller's pale complexion pinked under the sun, and after some time in Afghanistan his strawberry blond hair gave way to a grizzly, paprika-colored beard.

A few weeks into their deployment, Miller and Ody went on a mission with the MARSOC team. It was zero dark thirty. They were pressed into the Chinook helicopter with about two dozen other Marines. They had the spot closest to the ramp so the dog could stretch out and lie down. Miller's 90-pound rucksack was weighing down on him, pinching off his circulation as he crouched on the floor. When the Chinook lowered and they went to make the short drop to the ground, Miller could barely feel his legs.

Into the dark they jumped. Then they ran under the loud whir and rush of the blades that kicked up dust and rocks and, like a hurricane, hit them hard in the face. As they started to move forward, an air support assault erupted around them. The sound was deafening. As a C-130 shot down on them from above and the rush of bodies swarmed around them in the dark, Ody pulled at his leash, practically dragging his handler along, desperate to get away. The dog was freaking out.

Miller tried to calm Ody. First he offered the dog a Kong and then the tug toy he always carried on missions. But the dog refused them, and he wouldn't focus on anything. Instead he milled about aimlessly. He showed no interest in sniffing or investigating anything around him. Ody was in a state of fear and shock.

Miller kept an eye on Ody through his NVGs as they continued with the mission. But even while just moving from one point to the next, Ody kept trying to walk underneath Miller and move against his legs. When Miller took a knee, Ody pushed at him with his paws, trying to dig underneath him, to get to the only place he seemed to feel safe.

When they got back to Leatherneck, Miller took Ody to the vet right away. He was told to keep the dog content for the next few days, to just let him relax. Ody was locked up the whole night and all the next day. He wouldn't eat, he wouldn't sleep, he wouldn't even relieve himself. He finally started to relax the following day, and spent most of his time in Miller's bed.

But Ody didn't show much sign of improvement beyond that. The trauma from that night didn't leave him. He was jumpy around anyone other than his handler. Miller worried that Ody might bite someone, which, for a dog as easygoing as Ody, meant he was still very afraid.

Despite their poor performance during the mission, the MARSOC team wanted to keep the dog team around. Miller and his team leader decided that Ody should get a three-week retraining session. Their goal was to slowly and gently rebuild the dog's confidence. Each week they introduced a new kind of weaponry at the range, from pistols to rifles, from machine guns to RPGs and mortars, ramping up the noise volume with each weapon. On base Ody still proved to be a solid detection dog. He did well on every search drill. So they decided to try a low-intensity mission, a basic foot patrol during daylight. But as soon as they stepped off the base and outside the wire, Ody tensed up, all his skittishness returning. He knew he was leaving the place where he felt safe.

Miller could have tried another night mission with Ody, but MARSOC used a lot of mortars and rockets. When he asked himself if it was worth the risk, Miller knew the chance of doing more harm than good loomed too large in the end. Ody's lack of confidence was too big a risk factor, both for him and for the Marines on their missions.

The pair returned to Fort Rucker. Miller could see the difference in his dog as soon as they drove up to the kennels. He was as happy as a kid on Christmas. Ody knew he was home. Miller was confident that Ody would be a superb garrison dog, guarding a base and the troops. He just wasn't meant for war.

part six

what happens
when wars end

Many an American boy will survive this war and be restored to his family because some dog gave him warning of an enemy in time to seek cover, or sought him out as he lay helplessly wounded in some jungle thicket. Time and again these dogs have proved their worth in saving human life.

—Clayton C. Going, *Dogs at War*

63

In World War II, it is said that war dogs saved 15,000 men. In Vietnam, dogs were credited with saving the lives of 10,000 men, but many handlers who served there feel that this number is grossly underestimated.

How many lives dogs have saved in Iraq and Afghanistan won't be tallied until years from now. How high that number will be compared to past wars, one cannot say. But, as just one example of one dog team on one tour of duty, Technical Sergeant Justin Kitts and his dog Dyngo's detection work in Afghanistan secured the lives of 30,000 US, host nation, and coalition forces. For that Kitts received the Bronze Star in 2011.

In another example, Marine Core Gunnery Sergeant Justin Harding supervised a team of 17 Improvised Explosive Detector Dog (IEDD) handlers and 13 detection dogs on a seven-month tour in Afghanistan. Harding calculated that, during that time, his teams were responsible for finding approximately 500 IEDs. While he is infinitely proud of that number, Harding believes that even if only one dog had found only one bomb in the entire seven months, that would have been enough. At the very least, he figures, one bomb found would have equaled one Marine's life saved.

Equally impossible to tally are the lives that have been recovered, even in some small way, by a dog's healing presence, on a battlefield or in a wounded warrior treatment center.

The numbers are important because they represent human lives, but, from war to war, these very numbers are often forgotten. It is unfortunate, but this has already happened in the United States after World War II and after Vietnam. The value of war dogs has been lost as often as it has been found.

The events usually go a little something like this. The United States engages in a conflict. Someone, a person or group, with great resilience and spirit, petitions the military to adopt a canine fighting force, touting their many lifesaving skills. Someone in a position of power gives an order, and a small contingent of dogs is procured, trained, and deployed. Once in-country, the dogs prove to be of great value on the battlefield and save many lives. Next comes an "urgent need" request from the combat arena: "Send more dogs!" And so efforts are pooled and handlers and dogs are trained with intensity and speed. Sometimes compromises are made, sometimes shortcuts are taken, but more dogs are sent to war. The military parades the dogs' successes, the media seizes upon their stories, and headlines capture the hearts of civilians at home.

Then the war slows down and eventually ends. The tremendous canine force is scaled back, as are the combat-ready aspects of the dog programs, until they are virtually nonexistent. That is the distinct US war dog history: building to a great success that is later shelved and forgotten, only to be rebuilt again when the need arises. It's a precedent that created the kind of disadvantage no one fully realized until 2004, when it was time to send the dogs back to war, so many years after Vietnam.

Ron Aiello, the Marine handler who served in Vietnam with his scout dog Stormy, remembers how the canine program was dismantled after the war. First they got rid of the Marine Corps scout dogs, the mine dogs, and the booby-trap dogs.

Then the Army got rid of its tracker dogs. All canine combat readiness disappeared. He knew then it was a mistake.

After 9/11 happened and the Iraq War began, Aiello watched the news reports on television and saw military dogs working checkpoints or sniffing cars as they crossed gates. It infuriated him. He found himself shouting at the television set, "Have them out on patrol! Use them for IEDs!" But he knew those dogs weren't trained for that kind of work. He knew that building up those kinds of programs again from scratch would take years.

There are many parallels to draw between the wars in Iraq and Afghanistan and the one in Vietnam. Like the war in Vietnam, the wars in Iraq and Afghanistan have not been popular, and there is a rush to push our military's attention elsewhere. As the United States closes shop on two wars, the urgent need for dogs is already diminishing and will likely continue to lessen over time.

In response, the MWD program is already downsizing its number of combat-ready dogs. All branches of the military are seeing budgetary cuts. The programs that produced the "Dog Surge" of the mid-2000s—the Marine Corps' IEDD and the Army's TEDD—have already reduced their numbers and will certainly be disbanded. The need for dogs has not been extinguished, but it is no longer urgent. As one of his final acts as program manager at Lackland before retiring, Sean Lulofs was ordered to investigate cutting the program by one-third. In fact, he found a way to cut it in half.

64

There's no way that what happened in 1975 would happen now. The US military will never again leave its dogs behind as it did in Vietnam. This is in part because of the government's interest in monitoring the dogs' exit from the military, manifested in Robby's Law, but also because there is simply too much public visibility for such gross neglect to exist on such a grand scale. But just how far the programs will diminish, and whether or not the war dog lessons of these conflicts will be remembered, remains to be seen.

Aiello sees the troop drawdown, the program cuts, and the thinning of dog teams, and he sees the heavy curtain of past mistakes dropping again.

But he and handlers like him are the ones now building memorials and keeping track of handlers and dogs KIA. Their memory is institutional, and it is long. And just as Aiello and his handler buddies from Vietnam followed in the footsteps of the World War II handlers, so too will the war dog handlers of Iraq and Afghanistan.

When, in 2010, Gunnery Sergeant Justin Harding was with his team of IEDD handlers and dogs in Afghanistan, they made a stop at Camp Dwyer, one of the Marine Corps' largest military bases in the country, so the handlers could take their dogs to the veterinarians there. While they were waiting on base with their dogs, a lance corporal they didn't know approached them. This Marine had been with a unit in Marjah where the fighting had been especially fierce. The young man had returned to Dwyer looking battle-shocked, worn, and grief-stricken. The Marine had just lost some of his friends, but he wanted to thank the handlers and their dogs. "You know, you saved our lives," he said, "and I'm sure not all of you will come back."

Harding's infantry handlers, who hadn't yet been out on patrol, didn't know how to respond. Harding will never forget watching that young Marine, who was battered and damaged and already showing signs of the scars he'd likely carry for a lifetime, walk up to the handlers with tears in his eyes and reach out to shake their hands. In that moment, he was overcome with the certainty that being in Afghanistan with the dogs was the best thing he could have done to save lives in this war.

part seven

home again, home again

My little dog—a heartbeat at my feet.

—Edith Wharton

The good Lord in his ultimate wisdom gave us three things to make life bearable, hope, jokes and dogs, but the greatest of these was dogs.

—Robyn Davidson

65

Marine Corporal Eric Roethler was back at Camp Lejeune, North Carolina, after being deployed in Afghanistan. He'd just gotten called into the head shed where the staff had their offices. They wanted to talk to him about taking on a new dog, the dog he would take downrange with him when he went back over. When Roethler heard which dog they intended to give him, he was thrilled. "Heck yes," he told the staff sergeant. "I would love to take him as my dog." It was a big pat on the back, you could say, being given the responsibility of this particular dog.

Roethler had just spent his deployment with an eight-year-old German shepherd named Kito who'd already been downrange three times. Their rapport had come naturally, their communication had been smooth and fluid the whole way through. But as soon as Roethler had the leash of this new dog in his hands, he knew he had a challenge. He was having a hard time clicking with this dog, who was smart, stubborn, and used to having things go his way. When Roethler told the dog to go one way, he went the other way because that was just what he wanted to do.

From the outside, it may have seemed like 21-year-old Roethler had something to prove. He was working with another seasoned dog, a dog who had proven himself in training, and a dog who had married up well with his last handler. It was not that Roethler lacked confidence or that he wasn't ready to trust this dog. Maybe part of the issue was that this dog had been so close with his previous handler. Or maybe it was that the dog's former handler had been Roethler's corporal in Afghanistan. And that corporal hadn't just been any other Marine—it was Joshua Ashley. And this dog was Sirius, Ashley's dog.

Roethler had been in Afghanistan with Ashley the summer Ashley was KIA. The night Ashley died, Roethler and another Marine corporal were in the same area of operation, stationed at a MARSOC base. It was the middle of the night, and Roethler was gearing up with the Marine corporal for a mission when one of the team chiefs approached them. "Hey, I want to let you guys know that a dog handler got hit," he said. The chief didn't know who it was or if that man was alive or dead. He just wanted to let the handlers know that one of their own was down.

Roethler and his friend didn't believe it could be any of their guys. The hit had happened in Zombalay, and none of their guys was supposed to be on missions there. But when the chief came back and told them the handler's initials, they started to piece it together. It had to be Ashley.

Roethler went out on the mission that night and did his job no better or worse than he would've any other night. But there wasn't a moment that Ashley wasn't in the back of his mind.

Before Ashley was killed, Roethler had been able to watch him work Sirius in Afghanistan while they were training with the MARSOC guys. He'd seen what a solid detection dog Sirius was. He could tell what a good team they were.

But now it was September 2012. Ashley had been killed in action in July. It was time for Sirius to have a new handler.

After about a month of working with Sirius at the Lejeune kennels, things improved between Roethler and the dog.

In January 2013, they traveled together to Yuma for their pre-deployment training. Sergeant Charlie Hardesty and Staff Sergeant Lee McCoy, the same instructors who had coached Ashley through the March class the year before, were still there. It threw them a little to see Sirius come through again, but it was also like they got a little piece of Ashley back.

One afternoon, Roethler and Sirius were running drills in McCoy's lane, searching the compound's exterior. This drill was one of McCoy's specialties. There was nothing for the dog to find there, just a visual plant for the handler. There was no associative odor, so if they were going to find the bomb, it wouldn't be Sirius's nose but his handler's eyes that would catch it.

Roethler had his weapon raised and was using the scope on his rifle to scan the area. Sirius was out in front, sniffing and searching the ground. And then, through the lens, Roethler spied something glittering in the gravel. And no sooner did he raise his head to take another look and call back his dog than Sirius sat right in the middle of the road, turned his head back, and stared straight at him. The dog turned back again to look in the direction of that shiny material and then looked back again at his handler. Somehow he'd picked up on that IED plant and was letting his handler know there was something up ahead and he didn't like it.

McCoy let out a low whistle and turned to Roethler. "That's a solid dog right there," he told him. After that day, Roethler felt a difference in the relationship between him and Sirius. That was the day their bond took root.

When they're not working, Sirius is as gentle as a big teddy bear. He only wants to get petted and lie around. But when he and Roethler are working, he's still the same hardheaded dog. His stubborn streak is still strong. Just like Ashley's was. They

Marine Corporal Eric Roethler and MWD Sirius wait to board an aircraft aboard a multipurpose amphibious assault ship in March 2014.

Photo by Specialist 1st Class R J Stratchko

were exactly the same way, obstinate and hardheaded, wanting to do everything their own way. But, as Roethler said, "That is why they were such a good team." And every time that streak shows in Sirius, Roethler shakes his head, chuckles, and thinks about Ashley.

Roethler and Sirius were set to head to Afghanistan sometime in 2014. Roethler said at at the time that he felt 100 percent ready. He didn't worry that what had happened to Ashley would happen to him. "You can't live your life in fear," he said. "You think of the good, forget the bad." Roethler is almost defiantly proud that he took over Ashley's dog. And he has put all the faith he has in Sirius, a commitment that he feels the dog has earned. "First thing is trust your dog. You trust your dog, you follow him where he goes. If you don't trust your dog, you need to rethink your situation. You should have total faith to trust and walk behind him."

66

It was just about six o'clock when Matt Hatala met his mother in a Target parking lot in Waverly, Iowa, so they could swap cars. He traded her the keys to his diesel truck, a 2006 Chevy, and she handed over the ones that went with the borrowed Pontiac Vibe. When Hatala had realized how much gas it was going to take to drive his truck down to South Carolina, his mother called up a car salesman she knew at a local car dealership. As soon as he heard what her son was doing and why he needed a car, he'd arranged to get Hatala one for free.

Hatala threw his clothes into the hatchback and hugged his mother good-bye. Then he was on his way, with nothing but the June night and open road in front of him. He pushed his foot down and drove about as fast as the little Pontiac Vibe would go.

His first stop was Peoria, Illinois, to pick up Keegan Albright, another dog handler who had been in Afghanistan. They drove through the night until they reached Indianapolis, Indiana, where they met up with Shea Boland, the Marine who'd been Hatala's point man during all his patrols in Afghanistan. Pumped up on energy drinks and the buzz of reunion, the guys spent the whole time talking, taking turns napping, and driving. They hadn't been together since Afghanistan. They'd all gotten caught up in their own lives, but for Hatala, inside the small space of that car, it felt like no time had passed at all. He was back with his brothers and they'd be with him all the way to the kennels in South Carolina. They were going to get Chaney.

After Hatala got back from his tour in Afghanistan, he left the Marines. And even though he was home and employed, he was struggling. His job wasn't what he wanted it to be, things weren't going the way he planned. But then he had gotten a call that let him know that his request to adopt the bomb-sniffing dog he'd had with him in Afghanistan had been approved. The news that he could pick up his dog had filled him up with a kind of lightness he hadn't felt in a long time.

When they finally arrived at the kennels, Hatala just wanted to get his dog. After he filled out all the final paperwork and they waited for someone to bring Chaney out of his kennel, Hatala's excitement started to twist into a jittery ache. He hadn't laid eyes on Chaney since September 2011. A gap of nearly two years had gotten between them. In that time,

Chaney had been paired up with other handlers and redeployed to Afghanistan. Hatala's small worry that his old partner might not remember him started expanding.

Then Hatala saw Chaney, ambling along with another handler coming toward them. The dog's eyes seemed to take them in, but he didn't get excited at the sight of his old friends. It was like Chaney couldn't tell who Hatala was. Hatala could hardly blame him. He'd grown a beard, he'd gained a little weight, and he wasn't wearing his uniform. But then his old partner had changed too. Chaney wasn't quite the hulking mass of black dog that Hatala had pictured in his mind. He'd lost a bit of weight, and though still a large dog, he didn't seem quite so big anymore. His paws were white and his beard had grayed.

Hatala gave a good loud call of "Chaney!" The reaction was immediate. Chaney went nuts, pulling and straining to get to him. Relief flooded Hatala. His dog knew him. In all their time together, Chaney had proven himself a mellow and well-mannered dog. The only thing that ever really riled him up was a cat. So when Hatala saw Chaney respond to the sound of his voice, he knew his dog not only remembered him—he was incredibly happy to see him.

They handed Hatala Chaney's leash and that was it. He had his dog back. The guys climbed into the car, their mission accomplished. Boland rode in the back with Chaney. They had to fold down the right side of the backseat to fit in his crate, broken down into halves so it resembled a big white bathtub, almost overtaking the car. Chaney lounged comfortably. When he moved around, his giant head grazed the roof of the car. The now-four Marines drove back the way they had come, all of them finally together in a holy communion of brotherhood. It was bliss for Hatala. The only thing he wished was that their trip had lasted longer than four days.

When they first got back home to Iowa, Chaney followed his old handler everywhere he went, into one room and then the next, always by his side, just like he did when they were in Afghanistan. Every time Hatala went to the front door, Chaney was at his feet, face upward, eyes seeking as if he were asking "Where we going? Are we working?" But there were no patrols to make in Iowa, no drills to run.

There were also different rules. In Afghanistan, Chaney had gotten used to sleeping wherever he wanted, and usually that meant Hatala's cot and not alone on the square doggie bed on the floor. It took a few weeks for Chaney to settle into being a housedog, but he adjusted. He stopped following Hatala to the door. He got used to being left in the house.

When the excitement of bringing Chaney home to Iowa faded into something more like normal, Hatala realized just how profound an effect having Chaney back was having on him. He'd been sleeping better since Chaney moved in, he was less stressed—he was somehow more comfortable in his own home.

There was a while, at first, when having Chaney back felt surreal, like it hadn't really happened, as if the whole thing had just been a dream. But when he woke up each morning, Chaney was still there.

67

Colton Rusk's family home was always populated with dogs. All the Christmas photos of Colton and his two brothers have a dog or two crowded into the frame somewhere.

Colton was the middle child, a dark-haired little boy with a determined sense of independence. He never needed to be told to do his homework. He always took care of himself. He wanted to be a veterinarian when he grew up. That is, until he decided he wanted to be a Marine. And Colton always did what he set out to do.

Colton Rusk was born on September 23, 1990, and 20 years later, exactly to the day, he left for Afghanistan with Eli, his bomb-sniffing dog.

When Rusk called home, he had a way of talking to his mother, Kathy. He knew just what to say to set her at ease. He was more forthcoming with details when he spoke to his father, Darrell, but he was protective of his mother. After all, he had a big, red-hearted tattoo with the word *Mom* scrawled across the top of his right arm. From the way he sounded, Kathy could almost imagine that her son was somewhere else entirely, somewhere safe and happy. He sounded as if he were only away at summer camp instead of in a combat outpost in Afghanistan. And he always talked about Eli.

The last time he called home, the phone rang early on Sunday morning in Orange Grove, Texas. Rusk told his mom that the Marines of the 3rd Battalion, 5th Marine Regiment were moving to a safer location and that she shouldn't worry. He'd written a letter, he told her, and it was already on its way. He told her to keep an eye out for it. This was the first time Kathy had heard from her son in months. To have the sound of his voice come through so buoyant, so happy, and to hear him talking about how Eli was sleeping in his sleeping bag or taking up all the space on his cot all but pushed away her worry. That night Kathy went to sleep and actually got some rest.

The following Monday, December 6, 2010, Kathy and Darrell were notified that Rusk had been killed. Kathy's memory of that day is hazy, but she remembers hearing Darrell ask about Eli. Had Eli made it? Where was the dog now?

Kathy thought of the letter Rusk had sent and realized it was still on its way. It arrived the day before they buried him. At the top of the paper was a discernible smudge. Next to it Rusk had written: "Eli kisses."

Rusk's story, and the news that Eli had shielded his body after he was shot, had garnered a lot of attention. It did not happen often, but the Marine Corps offered the dog to the family.

Kathy never dreamed that they'd get Eli. And when the Marine Corps first contacted them about adopting the dog, Kathy and Darrell balked. They wanted him, yes, but how could they take him away from the other young men in Rusk's unit? They were assured that the dog couldn't stay with Rusk's unit. He would have to come back to the States and start all over again with a new handler before he could redeploy to Afghanistan. *If* he redeployed at all.

On February 3, 2011, the Rusks drove to Lackland Air Force Base to pick up Eli. Kathy was worried. It'd been months since they'd seen him, and she doubted that he would remember them. While they signed the adoption papers, questions ran through her mind: What if Eli was traumatized or didn't want to go with them? The small room they were waiting in felt even smaller in spite of the fact there were only a few people in there with them. When a Marine finally came in with Eli, from the moment the dog entered the room, Kathy was filled with a contented kind of certainty. The dog was meant to be with them, he was back with his family. She watched the way he strained at the leash to get closer to them, like he knew exactly who they were and he'd been waiting all this time to see them again.

After they drove the two hours back from Lackland, they brought Eli into the house and let him off the leash so he could explore his new home.

He made a beeline for Rusk's room and went right up onto his bed as if he knew exactly where he was going.

Every night Eli sleeps with Brady, the Rusks' youngest son, who was only 12 when Colton died. Eli sleeps not curled at the end of the bed but under the covers, wrapped in Brady's arms. He may shift around at night if he gets too hot, but he never moves until Brady falls asleep.

The Rusk family home has become something of a sanctuary for the Marines in Colton's unit. Every one of the young men in Rusk and Eli's unit has an open invitation to come and stay. A handful of Marines have already made this pilgrimage to call on the family of their fallen brother, to pay their respects, to visit, and to see Eli.

Kathy intuits that they wish to be alone with the dog, to visit with Eli in private. She senses they worry about her, her husband, and their other sons, as if they think somehow the family stopped living, too, when Colton died. "We tell them we want what is best for them, we want them to live their life to the fullest," she says. "We know Colton's life is over, but he would want them to live their life."

The Marines take solace in these visits and in the Rusk house. Some have stayed days. One even lived with the Rusks for a couple of months after he got out of the service. They act as big brothers to Brady. A few of them have taken to calling Kathy "Mom." That was hard for her.

More than three years later, there are still days when Kathy can't bring herself to get out of bed, and it's Eli who comes and finds her, who licks the tears off her face. The dog who lives in her house needs taking care of, and it's that need that pulls her up. Eli has his bad days too, when the ghosts of his past come to haunt him. To this day he doesn't like the sound of gunfire, and when there are fireworks going off, Kathy sees the change in him. She sees in his face that he's afraid. And then it's her turn to comfort him.

Every now and again Kathy comes across something that belonged to Colton, something that still carries his smell—an old shirt or his watch, the one he was wearing in Afghanistan that she keeps safely tucked away in a pouch in a cabinet. The Marines in Rusk's unit brought back all the toys and gear that Colton used with Eli, like his Kong, and gave it to the family. But those things are special, and the Rusks only bring them out on rare occasions. One day she caught Eli sniffing the cabinet, just sniffing and sniffing, and she couldn't think what he was after—until she remembered that Colton's watch was in the cabinet. Eli was sniffing out Rusk's scent. Now when Kathy finds Colton's things, she shares them with Eli. She drops down her hand to offer whatever she's holding to the dog. They inhale and remember together the young man they loved.

68

While ruminating on the loss of one of his longest-living pets, writer James Fallows remarked that "we take animals into our lives knowing that, in the normal course of events, we will see them leave. . . . Nothing lasts forever, and small animals are here for only a brief while." And yet, despite knowing that, we engage in this short-lived sojourn destined to mourn. We invite these creatures into our lives, again and again, knowing that however long their lives span, it will have been worth it in the end.

Eli is getting older. His joints ache a little. He's slowed down some. Kathy is more careful now not to let him wear himself out chasing tennis balls in the sun.

Before they went to pick Eli up and bring him home, Kathy wrote to the Marine Corps and asked that they please not neuter him because she wanted to breed him. They didn't want to make money off the puppies, she explained in her letter. They wanted to give Eli's puppies to the Marines in Rusk's unit. And so when they brought Eli home, they did so with his fatherhood abilities still intact.

Eli was mated with a chocolate Lab, and all 11 of the puppies born were black like him. Kathy had intended to give them to anyone from Colton's Marine battalion who wanted one, but so many of them were still in service. So, one puppy went to Colton's older brother Cody, who named the little dog Tough. Another went to Colton's cousins, who named the puppy Fern, after *Where the Red Fern Grows,* Colton's favorite movie. Still another puppy went to the casualty officer who helped the Rusk family through the worst of their grief following the notification of their son's death.

Kathy Rusk knows that Eli isn't going to live forever. She knows the dog will die, but she won't dwell on the thought, choosing instead to think of other things.

69

When his dog Aaslan retired, Sean Lulofs hadn't been able to adopt him. His wife had just had a baby, and Aaslan didn't have the right temperament for children. He kept tabs on the dog for a while. He knew about the family that had taken him in and where the dog was living. But around the time Aaslan would've been 14 years old, Lulofs stopped reaching out to hear news of his dog. It wasn't because he stopped caring, but he couldn't face the possibility that the dog might have died. So he just left it alone, preferring to keep the fantasy that he was alive and well.

Ron Aiello never found out what happened to Stormy, but when he went to that reunion for the World War II handlers, he met another Vietnam handler who had worked with Stormy after he left. He showed Aiello a photo of them together, taken in 1970. As far as Aiello knew, this was the last time there was any real record of her. Of all the fates that could have befallen his dog, Aiello prefers to believe that Stormy was killed in action rather than being handed over to the South Vietnamese Army, where she would likely have been euthanized. To think of that (or worse, to think she might've been killed and then eaten) fills him with anger.

After his tour ended, Aiello was certain he would never be able to have another dog again. It wouldn't be possible, he thought, that he could love another dog as much as Stormy, and it wouldn't be fair to another dog to always be comparing the next animal to her. But when his younger son pleaded for a dog, he made him a deal. He told his son that if he could keep a hamster alive for one full year, they would get a dog. Aiello thought it was a bet he couldn't lose. His son's first hamster hadn't lasted more than a few weeks. But the next hamster made it one year. A promise was a promise. So Aiello took his son to the pound and they adopted a shepherd-Lab mix called Sampson. Aiello grew to love this dog. It wasn't as hard as he thought it would be.

The hamster died exactly one week later, perhaps knowing he had served his purpose. Or, Aiello reasoned, the new big dog in the house had frightened the little thing to death. Either way, a dog had found its way into Aiello's home and into his heart again. Somehow, there had been room. There is always room.

acknowledgments

My father told me (often) to count my blessings, so here they are: my mother, Sheila; my father, Meyer; and my sister, Gail.

When it comes to this book, however, offering thanks must begin with Tom Ricks. For while I found the photo that set me on the war dog path, the journey that followed would not have been possible without Tom's encouragement. He recognized a good idea and then gave me full rein over it, and for this, I'm forever in his debt. If it was Tom who opened the reporting door, then it was Chris Jakubin who shepherded me through once I was on the other side. As my war dog mentor, he not only gave me his time but also his trust, going above and beyond to make sure I was connected with the best in the business, linking his reputation to mine.

After more than four years reporting on war dogs, I feel privileged to be a part of the military working dog community and all the communities—private, professional, and familial— that surround it by extension. I will always admire their fierce commitment to the dogs—it is selfless and without end. I owe thanks to so many people, among them: Bill Childress, Mike Dowling, Master Sergeant Kristopher Reed Knight, Captain John Brandon Bowe, Antonio Rodriguez, Sean Shiplett, Joel Burton, Sean Lulofs, Ron Aiello, and Richard Deggans; Bill Krol and Lisa Yambrick of American Vet Dogs; and the handlers who run the Military Working Dogs Facebook page. And for the men and women, some of them handlers, who for various reasons couldn't take credit by name for the help they gave me but offered it anyway, I'm grateful. In many ways I feel as though they gave me pieces of themselves around which I simply put words.

I do not know where this book would be without the creative and wonderful team at Macmillan, though I do know how lucky I am to have had the erudite and discerning Elisabeth Dyssegaard as my editor. She appreciated what I appreciated about these dogs and their handlers, and with kindness and knowing saw how to best bring their stories full circle. Special thanks to Donna Cherry for organizing the many facets of this book's production and to Bill Warhop, who copyedited the manuscript and whose line-by-line comments gave me much-needed encouragement in the last and most grueling phase of editing this book. I also wish to thank Lauren Dwyer-Janiec and Christine Catarino for their amazing work getting *War Dogs* out into the world. And for this special edition of *War Dogs*, many thanks to Thea Feldman for her work and to the patient and gracious Alan Bradshaw for overseeing all its pieces and parts.

Whatever challenges this book brought with it, I never took them on alone, for I had the counsel of Esmond Harmsworth, my brilliant and uncompromisingly lovely agent. I will always be thankful—and better off—for the guidance and support he offered.

Thanks to Ali Rhodes, Jared Mondshein, and Rick Carp, who all contributed their time and talent—fact-checking, transcribing, hunting down the most reluctant of contacts and most obscure details of military history—helping to guard against error, ultimately ensuring this book was better and smarter.

I am—and will always be—eternally grateful for the friendship of David Rothkopf. He was always there to remind me that the sky was not falling after all. I don't know where I would be without his humor and unflagging support. The crew at *Foreign Policy* magazine, a brilliant and wickedly funny band of creatives who are still relentlessly encouraging of my war dog endeavors, will always have my admiration and adoration—chief among them my friend Ben Pauker and my colleague Ty McCormick.

Thanks must be paid to Karin Tanabe, Jeremy Berlin, and Jennie Rothenberg-Gritz, who are not only among my dearest friends but are exceptional writers. Each of them provided insight, reassurance, and edits when I truly needed them most. And I am especially thankful and happy that my cousins Benjamin and Andrew Horowtiz offered their good thoughts and suggestions for this special edition of *War Dogs*.

Book writing was, at least as I experienced it, a sometimes terribly solitary exercise. But because of these friends, I was never lonely: Rachel Wozniak, Chris Wozniak, Michal Mizrahi, Jessica Pavone, Claire Bohnengel, Brandon Van Grack, Sarah Longwell, Erica Sandler, Molly Smith, Kyle Kempf, Nick Vilelle, Mitchel Levitas, James Fallows, Deborah Fallows, and, of course, Mike Fallows, and most especially my Great-Uncle Benny, who was the very best kind of friend.

glossary

II-MEF   II Marines Expeditionary Force

allied forces   armies from different countries fighting on the
                      same side in a war

al Qaeda   militant Islamic extremist organization founded
                      by Osama bin Laden

asymmetric weapons unequal fighting resources; for example, in
                      a conflict, one side might have tanks, fighter
                      jets, and all kinds of rifles, while the other has
                      homemade bombs

Ba'ath Party   the ruling political party in Iraq during the time
                      of Saddam Hussein

citadel   fortress

COSC   Combat and Operational Stress Control

CPTSD   canine posttraumatic stress disorder

DOD   Department of Defense

downrange   in a combat zone

EOD   explosive ordnance disposal; explosive disposal
                      teams safely detonate any live explosives that are
                      discovered

FINEX   final exams for the Inter-Service Advanced Skills
                      K-9 Course

FOB   forward operating base

garrisons   places where troops are stationed

hard knock   going full force into a house or other building

IED   improvised explosive device

IEDD   Improvised Explosive Detector Dog

in-country	in foreign territory, especially a combat zone
insurgents	people who revolt against established authority or government
ISAK	Inter-Service Advanced Skills K-9 course, taught at the Yuma Proving Ground in Yuma, Arizona
JIEDDO	Joint Improvised Explosive Device Defeat Organization
KIA	killed in action
klick	a kilometer (approximately two-thirds of a mile)
MARSOC	Marine Corps Forces Special Operations Command
medevac	a helicopter used to evacuate the injured
MWD	military working dog
NVGs	night vision goggles
ordnance	military weapons
outside the wire	beyond the safety of a base or other support area
PT	physical training
PTSD	posttraumatic stress disorder
RPG	rocket-propelled grenade
ruck march	a forced march at a fast pace with a weighted backpack
SEAL	a member of the US Navy's elite special operations force; *SEAL* stands for sea, air, and land
SF	Special Forces; elite forces within each branch of the military
Taliban	extremist Islamic movement controlling Afghanistan
TEDD	Tactical Explosive Detection Dog
TSA	Transport Security Administration
TWA	Trans World Airlines
USAF	United States Air Force

Vietcong	guerrilla fighters with North Vietnam during the Vietnam War
YPG	Yuma Proving Ground
zero dark thirty	an unspecified time early in the morning, before dawn

THREE GOOD WORDS TO KNOW

Do all three words apply to military working dogs? You decide.

love	a feeling of strong affection for someone or something
loyalty	a feeling of strong support for someone or something
trust	a feeling of confidence in someone or something

notes

CHAPTER 3

12   *"The people of the United States and our friends and allies . . ."* President Bush Addresses the Nation, White House Press Release, March 19, 2003, http://georgewbush-whitehouse.archives.gov /news/releases/2003/03/20030319-17.html.

12   *Forty to 60 percent of all attacks started with an IED . . .* "Improvised Explosive Devices (IEDs)—Iraq," GlobalSecurity.org, http:// www.globalsecurity.org/military/intro/ied-iraq.htm.

12   *In early 2004, General James Mattis issued an order . . .* From interviews with Colonel Mike Hanson (retired) on January 24, 2013, and Major Jim Griffin (also retired) on January 30, 2013, who were given orders to look into this. Their Marine battalion was part of the first invasion into Iraq in 2003.

CHAPTER 5

17   *Lulofs was determined to mess up . . .* When Lulofs and Aaslan left Iraq, the bounty on their heads had been upped twofold to $20,000.

17   *The six-lane highway usually had more traffic . . .* Tony Perry, "Snipers Stalk Marine Supply Route," *Los Angeles Times,* December 28, 2006.

CHAPTER 19

55   *The canine nose is a masterful creation . . .* There are quite a few alternatives for the word *nose,* some more fitting in the context of dogs than others for obvious reasons. Thesaurus.com offers: "adenoids, beak, bill, horn, muzzle, nares, nostrils, olfactory nerves, proboscis, schnoz, smeller, sneezer, sniffer, snoot, snout, snuffer, whiffer . . ." http://thesaurus.com/browse/sniffer.

55   *The average dog has roughly 220 million scent receptors . . .* Mark Derr, *Dog's Best Friend* (New York: Henry Holt, 1997), 95.

56   *These bombs are potluck-style concoctions,* . . . Section 5-2, "Explosives Used for Training," Army Manual, Department of the Army, September 30, 1993, http://armypubs.army.mil/epubs/pdf /p190_12.pdf.

CHAPTER 21

60   *"dogs get distracted,* . . .*"* Henry Fountain, "Devices Go Nose to Nose With Bomb-Sniffer Dogs," *New York Times,* October 15, 2012, http://www.nytimes.com/2012/10/16/science/explosives-de tectors-aim-to-go-nose-to-nose-with-sniffer-dogs.html.

62   *And for Rogal, those extra seconds could mean* . . . Phone interview with Staff Sergeant Taylor Rogal, October 10, 2012.

CHAPTER 22

62   *A signature feature of the bloodhound* . . . Bloodhounds have even more sensory receptors/olfactory cells in their nose than most breeds of dogs. "Underdogs: The Bloodhound's Amazing Sense of Smell," *Nature,* PBS series, original airdate January 29, 2006, http://www.pbs.org/wnet/nature/episodes/underdogs/underdogs -the-bloodhounds-amazing-sense-of-smell/350/.

62   *The bloodhound has on average 300 million scent receptors,* . . . Stanley Coren and Sarah Hodgson, *Understanding Your Dog For Dummies* (Hoboken: Wiley Publishing, Inc., 2007), 103; see also http://www.dummies.com/how-to/content/understanding-a -dogs-sense-of-smell.html.

CHAPTER 23

65   *For one thing, most dogs (depending on the breed)* . . . Alexandra Horowitz, *Inside of a Dog: What Dogs See, Smell, and Know* (New York: Scribner, 2009), 124.

65   *It reflects light, which helps dogs see* . . . Andrea Seabrook, "Why Do Animals' Eyes Glow In The Dark?" NPR.org, October 31, 2008, http://www.npr.org/templates/story/story.php?storyId=964 14364.

65   *Dogs' eyes also have more light-sensitive cells,* . . . "How Well Do Dogs See At Night?" *Science Daily,* November 9, 2007.

65   *In 2002, the Department of Zoology at Tel Aviv University* . . . Irit Gazit and Joseph Terkel, "Domination of Olfaction over Vision in Explosives Detection by Dogs," *Applied Animal Behaviour Science* 82, no. 1 (June 3, 2003): 65–73.

65   *to see whether a dog relies more on his nose or his eyes . . .* The Israel
       Defense Forces (IDF) have an extremely powerful dog program. In
       many ways they have set the recent standard of war dog training.
       In the mid-2000s the US Marines sent a small contingency of dog
       handlers to train with IDF handlers. One of the more revolutionary
       training methods those handlers brought back and made standard
       was the "off-leash capability."

CHAPTER 30

87   *Things that even a medic might not know . . .* Interview with US
       Army Sergeant George Jay and Army Specialist William Vidal
       (from Bagram Airbase), June 20, 2012.

CHAPTER 35

104   *As Horowitz observes, it allows us to suppose that we are . . .* Alexan-
       dra Horowitz, *Inside of a Dog* (New York: Scribner, 2009), 57.

CHAPTER 38

110   *In fact, especially in relations to guarding duties, . . .* E. H. Rich-
       ardson, *British War Dogs: Their Training and Psychology* (London:
       Skeffington & Son, Ltd., 1920), 151.

111   *Konrad Lorenz, a preeminent zoologist . . .* Known as the father of
       ethology, the study of animal behavior, especially in nature, Lo-
       renz's most notable contribution is thought to be his work identify-
       ing the pattern of imprinting in the Greylag goose. Born and raised
       in Austria, much of his work came during Hitler's rise to power.
       That he was a willing and ardent member of the Nazi Party and
       contributed to the science of eugenics, however, is, in the discus-
       sion on dogs, perhaps best overlooked but not forgotten. He would
       later recant this affiliation and expressed regret, as he wrote, for
       having "couched my writing in the worst of Nazi-terminology."
       "Konrad Lorenz—Biographical," Nobelprize.org, http://www
       .nobelprize.org/nobel_prizes/medicine/laureates/1973/lorenz-bio
       .html. The quote is from *Les Prix Nobel en 1973,* Editor Wilhelm
       Odelberg, Nobel Foundation, Stockholm, 1974.

CHAPTER 39

118   *Anax would lose his right leg, but he would survive.* See : http://www
       .stripes.com/news/strong-bonds-link-military-dogs-handlers-1.157
       898#.Tps3vLsYymV.facebook

CHAPTER 40

119   *They've learned "to interpret human communication, . . ."* "Dogs
      Decoded," *Nova,* PBS documentary, original airdate November 9,
      2010, http://www.pbs.org/wgbh/nova/nature/dogs-decoded.html.

120   *It turns out, as Mills discovered, . . .* Anaïs Racca, Kun Guo, Kerstin
      Meints, and Daniel S. Mills, "Reading Faces: Differential Lateral
      Gaze Bias in Processing Canine and Human Facial Expressions in
      Dogs and 4-Year-Old Children," *PLoS ONE,* April 27, 2012, http://
      www.plosone.org/article/info%3Adoi%2F10.1371%2Fjournal.po
      ne.0036076.

120   *For instance, we know their company lowers . . .* J. K. Vormbrock
      and J. M. Grossberg, "Cardiovascular Effects of Human-Pet Dog
      Interactions," *Journal of Behavioral Medicine* 5 (October 11, 1988):
      509–17, http://www.ncbi.nlm.nih.gov/pubmed/3236382.

120   *. . . and greatly reduces the stress . . .* Ashley Balcerzak, "How Your
      Dog Helps Your Health," *Men's Health,* November 7, 2013, http://
      www.menshealth.com/health/how-dogs-make-you-healthy.

120   *In 2010, researchers at the Karolinska Institutet in Sweden presented
      a study . . .* Dr. Z, "How Owning a Dog Extends Your Life,"
      Stresshacker.com, November 17, 2010, http://www.stresshacker
      .com/2010/11/how-owning-a-dog-extends-your-life/; "People &
      Animals—For Life," 12th International IAHAIO Conference, July
      1–4, 2010, Stockholm, Sweden, http://www.iahaio.org/files/con
      ference2010stockholm.pdf.

121   *The idea is backed by something far . . .* Phone interview with Marc
      Bekoff, September 10, 2012.

CHAPTER 42

123   *"The War Dog," Richardson wrote, "has to have all fear of explosions
      and firing . . ."* E. H. Richardson, *British War Dogs: Their Training
      and Psychology* (London: Skeffington & Son, Ltd.,1920), 150.

123   *"Apart from this trained courage," he continued, "we can all recall . . ."*
      E. H. Richardson, *British War Dogs: Their Training and Psychology*
      (London: Skeffington & Son, Ltd., 1920), 151.

124   *"Dogs," she said, "have been known to shield wounded men . . ."*
      "Dogs and Horses Often War Heroes," *New York Times,* October
      17, 1917, http://query.nytimes.com/mem/archive-free/pdf?res=F2
      0F14FB385F1B7A93C3AB178BD95F438185F9.

124   *The sergeant who finally had to pull the dog away with what the pa-
      per described as a "noose" . . .* Captain William W. Putney D.V.M.,
      USMC (Ret.), *Always Faithful* (New York: Free Press, 2001). No
      page number is available; it is included in the book's glossy insert,

a scan of a clipping from the author's "hometown paper, the *Farm-ville Herald*." No date is given.

125   *Nemo lost an eye, but both dog and handler* . . . "War Dogs Remembered," The United States War Dog Association, http://uswardogs memorial.org/id16.html.

125   *Private First Class Rusk* . . . Rebecca Frankel, "Rebecca's War Dog of the Week: Eli, Brother and Protector, Goes Home," ForeignPolicy .com, February 4, 2011, http://ricks.foreignpolicy.com/posts/2011 /02/04/rebeccas_war_dog_of_the_week_eli_brother_and_protec tor_goes_home.

CHAPTER 43

128   *It shattered the bone in the front part of his nose* . . . This description of Bronco's injuries comes from the vet who treated him at Bagram Airfield and operated on him twice, Captain Katie Barry, Facebook message, dated January 9, 2013.

CHAPTER 46

139   *They managed to get Ashley to Camp Leatherneck,* . . . A handler at Camp Lejeune, who wished to remain unnamed, confirmed the events as Josh's father described them to me, relaying the details as they were circulating at Camp Lejeune, II-MEF home station.

CHAPTER 47

141   *Marine Corporal Keaton Coffey died on May 24* . . . When the military pronounces someone killed "during combat operations," it makes for an entirely vague and unsatisfying qualifying of the account of someone's death. It's the description that came with the military death notices for Coffey, Brazas, and Ashley.

CHAPTER 48

146   *But that night was the only night she went home* . . . E-mail correspondence from Captain Katie Barry sent in early October 2012 from her new station in Germany.

CHAPTER 49

146   *Bruno reared up on his hindquarters, teeth showing, mugging for the camera* . . . Jeff Donn, "Soldiers Find Loyal Companions in War Dogs," Associated Press, NBC, August 12, 2007, http://www.nbc news.com/id/20151076/ns/health-pet_health/t/soldiers-find-loy

al-comrades-war-dogs/#.U3GQHC9RHyx. Some records incorrectly state that Bruno was killed in this attack. Master Sergeant (Ret.) Joel Burton confirmed that this was not the case. He wrote to me on September 27, 2012, that three dogs were wounded in this attack—Flapoor, Bruno, and Kevin all survived. The 341st Training Squadron at Lackland Air Force Base is responsible for keeping the records as mandated in Robby's Law. Burton, who was stationed at Lackland for eight years, was responsible for maintaining this document that tracks MWDs (from all branches) as he puts it, "from cradle to grave."

147   *Blood ran in a fast current* . . . Corporal Micah Snead, "Military Working Dog, Marine Stick Together Through Battle, Injuries," Leatherneck.com, February 7, 2006, http://www.leatherneck.com/forums/archive/index.php/t-26186.html.

147   *Later, when they cremated him, they found leftover* . . . Interview with Charlie Hardesty, March 2012.

147   *Cann was one of 58 people killed in that 2006* . . . "Five Camp Lejeune Marines Killed in Iraq," Associated Press, http://www.militarytimes.com/valor/soldier/1459367. No publication date is listed, but given that it was a wire story, it was likely January 2006.

147   *The others told him he didn't have to do the extra work,* . . . Mike Dowling, "SGT Adam Leigh Cann—Semper Fi War Dog," post from his now defunct blog *K-9 Pride*, April 22, 2008, http://k9pride.wordpress.com/2008/04/22/sgt-adam-leigh-cann-semper-fi-war-dog/.

CHAPTER 50

148   *. . . camp kaiser:* . . . Mike Pitts, "First Marine Scout Dog Killed in Action," photographer and publication unknown, 1966, at US War Dog Memorial Site, http://uswardogsmemorial.org/id16.html.

149   *. . . Pyle's account of this day is short* . . . Ernie Pyle, *Brave Men* (New York: Henry Holt, 1943).

CHAPTER 51

151   *There is no* centralized *official record of handlers killed in action* . . . Master Sergeant (Ret.) Joel Burton confirmed that this was an accurate statement.

CHAPTER 52

153   *Until Cann's death in 2006, there was nothing in place to keep track* . . . Interview with Master Sergeant (Ret.) Joel Burton, January 2013.

154   *He also "mapped where on the human body bullets . . ."* C. J. Chivers, "Cataloging Wounds of War to Help Heal Them," *New York Times,* May 17, 2012.

155   *A consolidated database . . .* C. J. Chivers, "Cataloging Wounds of War to Help Heal Them," *New York Times,* May 17, 2012.

CHAPTER 53

159   *To avoid injury from the resulting shrapnel spray . . .* Peter W. Singer, "Robots at War: The New Battlefield," *The Wilson Quarterly,* Winter 2009, http://www.wilsonquarterly.com/essays/robots-war-new-battlefield.

159   *In the three weeks before the Army officially pushed out the 5-and-25 program . . .* Joseph Giordono, "New Army Program Aims to Put Soldiers on Higher Alert for IEDs" *Stars and Stripes,* May 25, 2005.

159   *As the rate of IEDs continued to increase, so did the Pentagon's efforts . . .* James Dao, "Afghan War's Buried Bombs Put Risk in Every Step," *New York Times,* July 14, 2009.

159   *Its sole purpose, and its many billions of dollars in funding . . .* Formerly the Joint IED Defeat Task Force founded in 2004: http://www.globalsecurity.org/military/agency/dod/jieddo.htm.

160   *JIEDDO spent upward of $19 billion pursuing numerous technological innovations . . .* Spencer Ackerman, "$19 Billion Later, Pentagon's Best Bomb-Detector Is a Dog," *Danger Room* blog, *Wired,* October 21, 2010, http://www.wired.com/dangerroom/2010/10/19-billion-later-pentagon-best-bomb-detector-is-a-dog/.

160   *After all the money spent and all the tools developed during those years, Oates said . . .* Spencer Ackerman, "$19 Billion Later, Pentagon's Best Bomb-Detector Is a Dog," *Danger Room* blog, *Wired,* October 21, 2010, http://www.wired.com/dangerroom/2010/10/19-billion-later-pentagon-best-bomb-detector-is-a-dog/.

160   *Barbero reported that the threat would not only persist . . .* Statement By Lieutenant General Michael D. Barbero, Director Joint Improvised Explosive Device Defeat Organization, United States Department of Defense, before the United States House of Representatives Committee on Appropriations Subcommittee on Defense, September 20, 2012, https://www.jieddo.mil/content/docs/20120920_JIEDDO_Statement_for_the_Record.pdf.

160   *"The IED and the networks that employ these asymmetric weapons . . ."* Otto Kreisher, "IEDs Replace Artillery As Battlefield's Biggest Killer, JIEDDO General Says," *Breaking Defense,* October 17, 2012, http://defense.aol.com/2012/10/17/ieds-replace-artillery-as-battlefields-biggest-killer-jieddo-g/.

CHAPTER 54

162   *By noon that day, two of the airline's pilots refused to fly* . . . Associated
       Press, "Bomb Explodes in Parked Plane," *Evening Independent* (St.
       Petersburg, FL), March 8, 1972; Richard Witkin, "Bomb Found
       on Jet Here After $2-Million Demand," *New York Times,* March 8,
       1972; Richard Witkin, "T.W.A. Jet Damaged in Las Vegas Blast,"
       New York Times, March 9, 1972; "Nixon Orders Tighter Air Secu-
       rity," *Daytona Beach Morning Journal,* March 10, 1972; "President
       Orders Tighter Security by U.S. Airlines," special edition, *New York
       Times,* March 10, 1972; Robert Lindsey, "Air Security Tightened to
       Meet Order by Nixon," special edition, *New York Times,* March 11,
       1972; *ABC News,* aired March 8, 1972; "1972: TWA Jet Explodes
       at Las Vegas Airport," *On This Day,* BBC, http://news.bbc.co.uk
       /onthisday/hi/dates/stories/march/8/newsid_4268000/4268151
       .stm.

163   *Federal Aviation Adminstration representative, Lieutenant General
       (Ret.) Benjamin Davis* . . . "Bomb on TWA Plane," *ABC News,*
       aired March 8, 1972, http://abcnews.go.com/Archives/video/marc
       h-1972-bomb-twa-plane-13078635.

CHAPTER 55

166   *And if you look at who those lobbyists were that pushed through
       those machines* . . . "TSA Oversight Part 2: Airport Perimeter Se-
       curity," Serial No. 112–75, July 13, 2011, http://oversight.house
       .gov/wp-content/uploads/2012/04/7-13-11-Subcommittee-on-Na
       tional-Security-Homeland-Defense-and-Foreign-Operations-Hear
       ing-Transcript.pdf.

CHAPTER 56

167   *Earlier that day, Army Sergeant John M. Russell* . . . "U.S. Soldier
       Charged with Murder in Iraq Shooting Deaths," CNN.com, May
       12, 2009, http://edition.cnn.com/2009/WORLD/meast/05/12
       /iraq.soldiers.killed/.

167   *He then forced the man from the car at gunpoint* . . . Rod Nordland,
       "Report Finds Lapses in Handling of G.I. Accused of Murders in
       Iraq," *New York Times,* October 20, 2009.

167   *The military police on the phone with the clinic said they* . . . Luis
       Martinez and Martha Raddatz, "Camp Liberty Shooting: Alleged
       Shooter's Dad Says Soldier 'Just Broke,'" ABC.com, May 12, 2009,
       http://abcnews.go.com/Politics/story?id=7565251.

CHAPTER 57

169   *Between 2007 and 2011, eight dogs made up the very first COSC dog therapy* . . . William Krol, "Training the Combat and Operational Stress Control Dog: An Innovative Modality for Behavioral Health," *United States Army Medical Department Journal: Canine Assisted Therapy in Military Medicine* (April–June 2012): 46.

173   *In urban areas of Iraq, dogs run wild* . . . Bushra Juhi, "58,000 Dogs Killed in Baghdad in Campaign to Curb Attacks by Strays," *Washington Post,* July 11, 2010, http://www.washingtonpost.com /wp-dyn/content/article/2010/07/10/AR2010071002235.html.

CHAPTER 58

174   *According to a 325-page report published in October 2009 investigating the incident* . . . Rod Nordland, "Report Finds Lapses in Handling of G.I. Accused of Murders in Iraq," *New York Times,* October 20, 2009.

175   *The 1 percent of Americans who have served in the US military make up 20 percent* . . . Margaret C. Harrell and Nancy Berglass, "Losing the Battle: The Challenge of Military Suicide," Policy Brief by Center for New American Security, October 2011. The policy brief's authors got these numbers from the Department of Defense and the Department of Veterans Affairs. It was of particular interest that the authors made a special note in the report that they intentionally "refrain from using the phrase 'commit suicide . . .' because the word 'commit' portrays suicide as a sin or crime . . . [and] contributes to a stigma that prevents individuals from getting help."

175   *"Suicide," as journalist Tina Rosenberg reported in September 2012* . . . Tina Rosenberg, "For Veterans, a Surge of New Treatments for Trauma," *New York Times,* September 26, 2012.

175   *But as Harold Baynes reported from France* . . . Ernest Harold Baynes, Animal Heroes of the Great War (New York: The Macmillan Company, 1925).

176   *"No longer dependent on a member of the family, a friend or a paid attendant* . . . Dorothy Harrison Eustis, "The Seeing Eye," *Saturday Evening Post,* November 5, 1927. To no great surprise the Germans, who proved ahead of the canine curve in most instances, were the first to use guide dogs, training them with innovation and then assigning them to soldiers who had been blinded in battle by mustard gas.

177   *By 1936, the school had paired dogs with 250 blind men* . . . "Guide Dog, at 10, Still Aiding Blind," *New York Times,* October 16, 1936.

CHAPTER 59

178   *As early as 1919, the US military brought dogs in as therapy tools for World War I* . . . Perry R. Chumley, "Medical Perspectives of the Human-Animal Bond within the Department of Defense," *The United States Army Medical Department Journal* (April–June 2012): 18–20.

178   *Instead she stayed on that bed, curled up with the young man* . . . Clayton G. Going, *Dogs at War* (New York: The Macmillan Company, 1945), 164–65.

179   *He improved so much that his recovery time exceeded* . . . Fairfax Downey, *Dogs for Defense: American Dogs in the Second World War 1941–1945* (New York: Dog for Defense, Inc., 1955), 114–115.

179   *"The Red Cross got me Patty, the swellest Irish Setter* . . .*"* Fairfax Downey, *Dogs for Defense: American Dogs in the Second World War 1941–1945* (New York: Dog for Defense, Inc., 1955), 117.

180   *In 1962, Levinson published an article on the phenomenon* . . . B. M. Levinson, "The Dog as Co-Therapist," *Mental Hygiene* 46 (1962): 59–65.

180   *In 2003 . . . Sandra Barker of Virginia Commonwealth University, reported* . . . Mark Thompson, "Bringing Dogs to Heal," *Time,* December 5, 2010.

180   *. . . 12 minutes of time spent with therapy dogs improved "heart and liver function . . ."* Major Arthur F. Yeager and Captain Jennifer Irwin, "Rehabilitative Canine Interactions at the Walter Reed National Military Medical Center," *The United States Army Medical Department Journal* (April–June 2012): 57–60.

180   *In tandem with this pilot program* . . . "Franken-Isakson Service Dogs For Veterans Act Passes Senate: Legislation To Help Wounded Veterans Included In Defense Authorization Bill," press release, July 24, 2009, http://www.franken.senate.gov/?p=press_release &id=592.

180   *. . . the federal government committed to spending several million dollars . . .* Janie Lorber, "For the Battle-Scarred, Comfort at Leash's End," *New York Times,* April 3, 2010, http://www.nytimes .com/2010/04/04/us/04dogs.html.

181   *Within a short time, they had their first trained service dog on staff* . . . Phone interview with Harvey Naranjo, January 27, 2013.

CHAPTER 61

186   *Dr. Walter E. Burghardt Jr., estimated* . . . James Dao, "After Duty, Dogs Suffer Like Soldiers," *New York Times,* December 1, 2011.

PART 6

191 *Clayton C. Going, Dogs at War* . . . Clayton G. Going, *Dogs at War*
(New York: The Macmillan Company, 1944), 3–4. This is a selec-
tion shared by Going but is excerpted from *The National Humane
Review of the American Humane Association;* no author is noted.

CHAPTER 64

196 *When, in 2010, Gunnery Sergeant Justin Harding* . . . Dan La-
mothe, "Afghanistan Drawdown Keeps Logistics Crews Busy,"
Marine Corp Times, June 11, 2012, http://www.marinecorpstimes
.com/news/2012/06/marine-logistics-afghanistan-equipment
-leaving-061012/.

index

Names in parentheses refer to handlers' dogs.

Aiello, Ron (Stormy), 27–33,
  194–6, 214–15
Air Force, 2, 7–8, 12–13
  Lackland Air Force Base, 25,
    37–8, 44, 106, 131, 152, 186,
    195, 210–11
  US Air Force (USAF) Academy,
    38–44, 47, 105, 121, 150,
    187
airport security, 161–6
al Qaeda, 3
America's VetDogs, 170
American Air Forces Convalescent
  Hospital (Pawling, New York),
  179
Anderson, Mike (Cezar), 163–5
Army, 2, 12, 21, 60, 67, 113, 166–7,
  175, 185, 187
  64th Medical Detachment
    (Veterinary Services), 143
  Buckley Air Force Base, 39,
    52–3, 83
  Combat and Operational Stress
    Control (COSC) Unit,
    170–4
  Dogs for Defense program, 3,
    28, 179
  Fort Carson Army Base, 62

Tactical Explosive Detection
  Dog (TEDD) program, 141,
  195
Ashley, Joshua (Sirius), 85, 93,
  96–100, 139–42, 155–6,
  202–5

Baer, Jon (Benny), 108
Barbero, Michael D., 160
Barry, Katie, 143–6, 150, 186
Baynes, Ernest Harold, 175–6
Beauchamp, Phil (Endy), 89–90,
  96–9
Bekoff, Marc, 107, 111, 121
Bin Laden, Osama, 3
bite-work training, 10, 46, 49–52
Boland, Shea, 134–5, 206–7
bomb dogs, 3, 13–14, 17, 42, 56–
  61, 65–6, 73–5, 154, 163–6,
  185, 193, 203, 206, 209
booby traps, 28, 75, 194
Bowe, John Brandon, 80–1, 85
Brazas, Sean, 141
British Air Regiment, 69
Brodsky, Michael J., 141–2
Brown, Terry (Vicky), 62–3
Burton, Joel, 152
Bush, George W., 12

Camp Baharia, 9, 16
Camp Dwyer, 196
Camp Leatherneck, 139–40, 149, 188
Camp Lejeune, 28, 201
Camp Liberty Stress Clinic, 166–7, 174
Camp Pendleton, 7, 148
Cann, Adam (Bruno), 146–8, 153
Carnell, Edward (Haus), 53–4
canine dominance and organization, 103–4
canine nose, 55–65, 76, 78, 130–2, 185
canine posttraumatic stress disorder (CPTSD), 185–7
canine teeth, 51–2
canine vision, 64–5
Carlson, Ted (Rambo), 50
Coast Guard, 12
Coffey, Keaton, 141
Combat and Operational Stress Control (COSC) Unit, 170–4
Connally, David (Brandy), 162
Creamer, Zainah (Jofa), 150
Curtis, Sabrina (Jessy), 185–6

deaths of MWDs and handlers, 2–3, 141–53
Department of Defense (DOD), 37, 152–3, 159
Dogs for Defense, 3, 179
Dog's Nose Program, 59
Doughty, Alyssa, 143, 145, 150

Eustis, Dorothy Harrison, 176–7
Explosive Ordnance Disposal (EOD), 11, 24, 60–1, 95, 99, 114, 117

5-and–25 tactical campaign, 159
Fallows, James, 212
Fallujah, 9, 16, 19–20, 153

Farnsworth, Joshua (Eesau), 9, 11, 16–19, 154
Ferrell, Kent (Zora), 139–40
FINEX, 87, 96, 100
forward operating base (FOB), 113, 149–50, 170
Frank, Morris, 176–7
Franken, Al, 180

Garcia, Eddie, 85
Gavin, Ciara, 46–8
Going, Clayton C., 191
guide dogs, 175–7
Gutierrez, Pascual, 105–7

Hardesty, Charlie (Robbie), 66–78, 85–8, 91, 94–6, 99, 142, 186, 203
Harding, Justin, 193, 196–7
Hatala, Matt (Chaney), 132–5, 205–8
Hilliard, Stewart, 37
history of Military Working Dogs (MWDs), 2–3
homemade explosives, 56
Hook, Sara, 182–3
Horowitz, Alexandra, 104
Howard, Kevin, 103–5, 107–8

Improvised Explosive Detector Dog (IEDD), 193, 195–6
improvised explosive device (IED), 3, 11–13, 17–18, 62–73, 127, 132–3, 159–67, 193, 195–6
Inter-Service Advance Skills K–9 (ISAK), 2, 66, 73, 81, 87, 139, 142, 147, 150, 155–6, 185, 187
interservice Iron Dog Competition, 44
Isakson, Johnny, 180

Jakubin, Chris, 37–48, 50, 52–5, 62–4, 93, 103, 105, 108–9, 121–2, 187

Joint Improvised Explosive
    Device Defeat Organization
    (JIEDDO), 159–60

Kaminski, Juliane, 118–19
Keilman, Christopher, 79–80, 86,
    91
Keller, Hellen, 157
King, William E., 178
Kitts, Justin (Dyngo), 6, 80, 94–6,
    98–9, 142, 150, 193
Knight, Kristopher Reed (Max), 67,
    82–7, 93–4

Lee, Dick A. Jr., 141
Lorenz, Konrad, 111
Lulofs, Sean (Aaslan), 7–11, 16–21,
    110, 112, 153–4, 195, 214
Lutenberg, John, 62–4

Maitland, Euphistone, 124
Maldonaldo, Jesse, 147
Mariana, John (Bronco), 126–32
Marine Corps, 2, 7, 12–13, 32, 124,
    139, 141, 148, 188, 194–6,
    204, 210, 213
    II Marines Expeditionary Force
        (II-MEF), 139
    Marine Corps Forces Special
        Operations Command
        (MARSOC), 139, 143,
        188–90, 202
Mattis, James, 12
McCombe, Pete, 70–2
McCoy, Lee (Spalding), 67, 85–92,
    96, 99–100, 203
Military Police Instruction
    Company, 81
Military Working Dogs (MWDs)
    and other war dogs
    Aaslan, 8–11, 18, 20–1, 112,
        153, 214
    Agbhar, 41–2
    Anax, 113–18

Benga, 43
Benny, 108
Bert, 106–7
Boda, 121–3
Boe, 166–74, 183–4
Bronco, 126–32
Bruno, 146–8
Budge, 169–70
Cairo, 3
Chaney, 132–5, 206–8
Duc, 13–15
Dyngo, 21–7, 80, 94–6, 98–9,
    142, 150, 193
Eesau, 16, 19
Eli, 125, 209–13
Endy, 89–90, 96–9
Fibi, 141
Flapoor, 146
Ginger, 42–3
Haus, 52–5
JaJo, 141
Jeny, 80
Jessy, 80, 185–7
Jofa, 150
Kaiser, 148
Kelly, 47–8
Layka, 141
Lex, 74–8, 85
Lucky, 124
Mack, 39–41, 44, 106
Max, 82–6
Nemo, 125
Nina, 141
Ody, 187–90
Oli, 40
Paco, 141
Rambo, 50–2
Robbie, 69–72
Sirius, 85, 93, 95–100, 139–40,
    156, 202–5
Spalding, 88
Stormy, 27–32, 194, 214
Taint, 37–42, 109
Teri, 60–2

Tosca, 143–5
    Turbo, 1–2, 80
    Uudensi, 67–9
    Vicky, 62–4
    Zora, 139–41
Miller, Donald Craig (Ody),
    187–90
Mills, Daniel, 119–20
Motz, William, 161–2

Najera, Cecilia (Boe), 166–74,
    183–4
National Guard, 12
Navy, 2, 12, 141
    SEAL team, 3
night vision goggles (NVGa), 8,
    88–90, 95, 97–8, 127, 189

Oates, Michael, 160
occupational therapist–dog
    handlers, 170–1, 181, 184
Operation Phantom Fury, 7

patrol base (PB), 26, 69, 126, 170
Peeler, John W. (Lex), 74–8, 85
physical training (PT), 66
Poelaert, Brendan (Flapoor),
    146–7
posttraumatic stress disorder
    (PTSD), 175, 180–2, 186
Pyle, Ernie, 149

Reese, Gregory, 60–1
Richardson, E. H., 110–11, 123–4
Roberts, Fred (Turbo), 1–2
rocket-propelled grenades (RPGs),
    14, 18, 22–3, 114, 189
Roethler, Eric (Sirius), 201–5
Rogal, Taylor (Teri), 60–2
Rusk, Colton (Eli), 125, 208–13
Russ, Dontarie R. (Uudensi),
    67–9
Russell, John M., 167, 174

Salazar, Alfredo (Kaiser), 148
Salisbury, Beth, 166, 168
Schmitt, William F., 162
scout dogs, 3, 28, 32, 148, 194
September 11, 2001, 3, 93, 163
Service Dogs for Veterans Act,
    180–1
South Vietnamese Army, 29, 33,
    214
Special Forces (SF), 7, 14, 126–7
Stone, William, 87, 91–2
Strader, Wayne (Rex), 164
Strong Point Haji Rahmuddin, 21

Tactical Explosive Detection Dog
    (TEDD), 141, 195
Taliban, 21, 24, 69–70, 74, 125
Tarwoe, Abraham, 141
therapy dogs, 166–84
Thorneburg, Robert (Nemo),
    124–5
tracker dogs, 62, 69, 74, 76–8,
    195
traffic control points (TCPs),
    16–17
TSA (Transport Security
    Administration) Bomb Dog
    Program, 163–6

Vest, George Graham, 101
Vidal, William, 143–5, 150
Vierig, Mark (Duc), 13–15
Vietnam War, 3, 13, 27–33, 146,
    148, 193–6, 214

Walter Reed National Military
    Medical Center, 169, 181–3
Warrior Transition Brigade's
    Wounded Warrior Service
    Dog Training Program,
    181–3
Whaley, Robbie (Boda), 122–3
Whittaker, Marc (Anax), 113–17

Wilson, Robert, 85
Wirt, Michael D., 154–5
World War I, 110, 124, 179, 179
World War II, 3, 33, 124, 149, 177,
    179, 181 193–4, 196, 214

Wrinkle, Christopher (Tosca), 143

Yuma Proving Ground (YPG), 2,
    26, 73, 77, 83, 89–90, 97–8,
    139, 155